God and the Snake-Child

Steve Eggleton

LION
CHILDREN'S

Published by Lion Children's
www.lionhudson.com
Part of the SPCK Group
SPCK, 36 Causton Street, London SW1P 4ST

ISBN 978 0 74599 792 6
e-ISBN 978 0 74599 795 7

First edition 2023

A catalogue record for this book is available from the British Library
Printed in Great Britain by Clays Ltd., March 2023

Contents

Chapter 1. Snakes in the Classroom 6
Chapter 2. Sacrifice. 13
Chapter 3. The Pilgrim Festivals .17
Chapter 4. The Great Feast. 21
Chapter 5. Siloam and Back. 28
Chapter 6. The Last Day of the Feast 35
Chapter 7. John Spots a Snakes' Nest. 45
Chapter 8. Jesus from Nazareth 53
Chapter 9. Secret Meeting 57
Chapter 10. Poisonous Snakes 70
Chapter 11. The Plot to Kill Jesus. 73
Chapter 12. Jesus Arrives in Jerusalem 78
Chapter 13. The Snake on the Pole 84
Chapter 14. Neeko and Josef Bury Jesus 90
Chapter 15. The Wait. 95
Chapter 16. Seismic Happenings 100
Appendix. Mrs Jakov's Spiced Cakes. 106

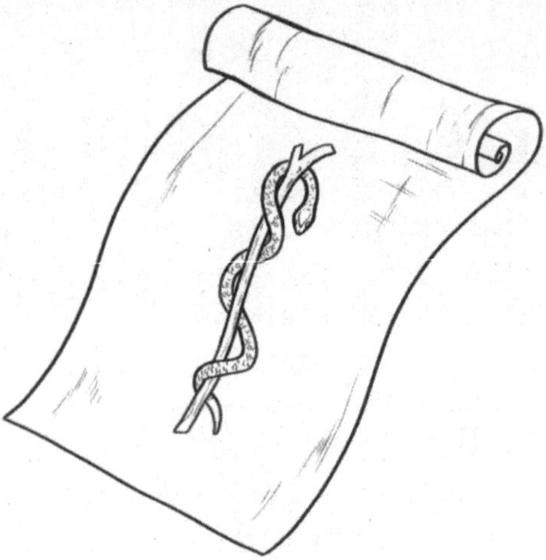

CHAPTER 1

Snakes in the Classroom

Neeko's mother had told him that, when he was tall enough to reach the knocker on Rabbi Jakov's door, she would allow him to walk to school on his own.

This morning, he was setting out for the first time through the narrow stone-paved streets of Jerusalem without Amoz, the family servant, by his side. He felt very grown-up.

Rabbi Jakov's house stood next to the synagogue. When Neeko got there, he was disappointed to discover that the door was already standing open. There was no need to use the knocker. He slipped inside to join the rest of the boys.

"Come on in, dear boy," said Rabbi Jakov. "Now let me see those hands."

Neeko stood looking up at the old man. He held out his hands for an inspection.

"Give them a wash, my boy, before we start work. We mustn't leave grubby fingermarks on the Holy Scriptures."

Neeko went to the big washing bowl. He washed his hands and dried them on the towel that hung nearby. Then he returned to the Rabbi for another inspection.

"That will do nicely. Now let's get started."

Neeko went to the cabinet where all the scrolls were stored. He carefully took out the fourth book of Moses and carried it to his desk. Gently unrolling the scroll, he found the place where he had finished the day before. Then he took a fresh writing-tablet and stylus and began to copy out the Hebrew characters into the smooth wax surface. There was something very special about starting work on a fresh writing-tablet.

Perhaps on this one, there will be no mistakes, he thought. *It will be perfect, right through to the end.*

He started at the top right-hand corner of the tablet and worked his way across toward the left. Some of the words he knew. Some he didn't yet understand, but he enjoyed copying these little squiggles that made up the Hebrew characters.

Rabbi Jakov came and looked over his shoulder.

"Read the words with me, my boy," he said, pointing with his beautiful silver reading-pointer.

Their two voices continued together. Old Jakov reading slowly and carefully, Neeko following uncertainly, stumbling over the more difficult words.

"So Moses made a snake out of bronze, and put it on a pole. Then, when anyone who had been bitten by a snake went and looked at the bronze snake, he lived."

The Rabbi rubbed his beard and looked closely at Neeko's work.

"One or two of your letters are not as beautiful as they might be, my boy," he said, pointing at the word "snake". "Let's try again. We'll copy this word seven times, until it is beautiful. Eh, my boy?"

So Neeko tried again and again: snake, snake, snake, snake, snake, snake, snake. He wrote slowly at first, but then with growing confidence, until the last one looked really good. It was almost as good as the one on the scroll.

Jakov will be pleased with this one, he thought. He jumped up from his desk and took his writing tablet to show the Rabbi. The old man looked at the row of snakes and chuckled.

"That's a proper little nest of snakes," he said. "Are they the poisonous ones that bit the people, or the good one that Moses made?"

Neeko looked up at the old man.

"I think they are mostly bad, except the last one. That's the one that made the people get well again."

"I will tell you the rest of that story later. It's a good one," said Jakov, smiling.

Toward the end of their morning lessons, the delicious smell of baking drifted into the classroom from Mrs Jakov's kitchen. This was the signal for the boys to finish their work, carefully put the scrolls away in the cabinet, and tidy up their things.

Rabbi Jakov sat down in his big chair, while all the boys sat on the wooden benches facing him.

"Today, I will tell you the story that young Neeko has been working on," began Jakov. "It's all about snakes. You can find this story in the fourth book of Moses.

"Our ancestors, the people of Israel, were travelling through the wilderness. They'd had a miraculous escape from Egypt, and God had faithfully provided them with food each day. Each morning little white flakes of bread-like stuff lay on the ground for the people to collect and use for food. They called it 'manna'. It was perfectly good, but the people were not happy. They grumbled against God, and against Moses.

"'You have brought us all this way, just to die in the desert,' they said. 'There's never enough water. We don't get to eat decent bread, and we are fed up with having to make everything from this miserable manna stuff.'

"Now God doesn't like to hear us grumbling, my boys. He wants his people to be full of thankfulness. Just remember that. It's very important." Then Rabbi Jakov continued the story.

"So God gave them something to think about. He arranged for lots of poisonous snakes to get into their tents, and among their things. The snakes bit the people, and many of them died.

"The people went to Moses and admitted that they had been wrong to complain.

"'We were wrong to speak against God, and against you, Moses,' they said. 'Please ask God to take these horrible snakes away.'

"So Moses went to God and asked him to take the snakes away from the people, but God had a better idea. He asked Moses to do something rather strange.

"'Moses,' he said, 'I want you to make a model of a snake. Fix it to a long pole, and stand it up high, where everyone can see it. Anyone who is bitten can look up at it, and they will be healed.'

"So Moses made a snake out of bronze and fixed it to a long pole and set it up high, where all the people could see it. And so it was, my boys," said Jakov, looking around at all the eager faces of his students.

"Anyone who had been bitten by those deadly snakes," he continued, "could look up at that snake on the pole and be healed."

The smell of baking from Mrs Jakov's kitchen was getting stronger. Jakov got up from his chair and leaned forward on his desk.

"So, here's a question for you, my boys," he said, wagging his reading-pointer at them. "Was it the snake that healed the people, or was it something else?"

Neeko's hand shot up.

"Well, what do you think, Neeko my boy?"

"I think it was God, Rabbi Jakov."

"Maybe, maybe, but if it was God, then why didn't he heal everybody – eh?"

There was silence in the room. Most of the boys were thinking about Rabbi Jakov's question. Some of them were thinking about cakes.

Mrs Jakov appeared at the door with a basket full of steaming spicy cakes. She stood and waited for her husband to finish his lesson. She knew better than to disturb him. She knew that there was often an important point to be made right at the end of his lesson.

Jakov looked from one face to another. He could see that he wasn't going to get an answer from the boys. This was a difficult question.

"Listen to me, boys," he said, leaning forward earnestly. "God is always looking for people who will trust him. That's what was going on here. Do you see? God didn't want to just simply heal everybody, or make the snakes disappear. He wanted his people to learn to trust him, even in the difficult times."

Jakov turned to his wife.

"OK, my dear. It's time we finished."

Mrs Jakov put the basket on Jakov's desk. She turned to the boys.

"Just one each, boys," she said. "Youngest first."

So each of the boys, under Mrs Jakov's watchful eye, came and leaned over the fragrant basket of cakes. The smell was intoxicating. Neeko took his time selecting a cake. Then he collected his things and prepared to leave the schoolroom.

He walked home slowly and thoughtfully. His mind was on what he had learned that morning.

"God of my fathers," he prayed, "I want to grow into a man who trusts in you."

When he arrived home, he was annoyed to discover that he had managed to eat his cake without even noticing.

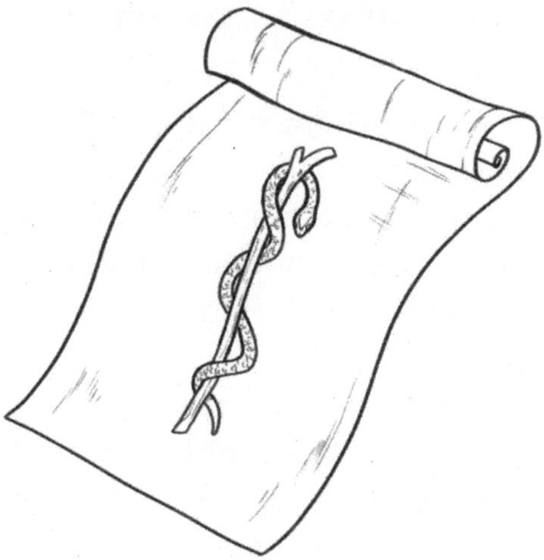

CHAPTER 2

Sacrifice

Neeko had been born into a family of Pharisees. These were people who believed that obeying God's law was the most important thing of all. It meant that even all the little rules and regulations, that had been added to the law over many years, had to be carefully followed too. As a boy growing up in a family of Pharisees, Neeko was expected to live in the same way. His life was always full of rules that had to be strictly obeyed.

For a Pharisee, the law and all the rules attached to it were even more important than the sacrifices that were offered in the great Temple, which stood high on the Temple Mount in Jerusalem. In fact, some Pharisees wanted to do away with the Temple worship altogether, and just have synagogues, where the law could be read and studied and taught.

Neeko often heard his father discussing these things with other men from the Pharisee movement. Sometimes, especially during the festival holidays, when nobody had to be up early for work in the mornings, the talking would go on late into the night.

"What do we need sacrifices for?" someone would ask. "If we keep the law, and never step out of line, we will always be clean and holy. God will be pleased with us."

"And if we keep up the washing routines," someone else would add, "surely that should be enough."

"All this sacrificing of animals, blood and mess everywhere. It's old-fashioned if you ask me."

"When our ancestors were in exile in Babylon, they didn't have the Temple. They managed without sacrifices. All they had was the Law and the Prophets. What more do we need?"

To begin with, Neeko found all this talk rather puzzling, but as he grew older, he began to understand more of the things about which his father and his father's friends constantly argued.

However, deep inside him, a strange tension was growing. Rabbi Jakov had helped him to see that there might be something more than just studying the Scriptures and obeying every little rule. Old Jakov really seemed to love God, and it showed in the gentle and loving way that he taught the boys. Neeko wanted that for himself. He wanted to have God as his friend, to walk and talk with him, just as Noah and Moses had done, and David and all the prophets.

One day, Neeko went with his father to watch the evening sacrifice at the Temple. All sorts of people gathered to watch the daily sacrifices, and pray as the smoke went up into the sky.

As they stood among the crowd, Neeko listened to all that was going on around him. He could hear people asking God to forgive them for the things that they had done wrong. Some people were crying and thanking God for his great mercy. Neeko knew that his family would never pray like that, nor any of his father's Pharisee friends.

As they walked back home after the sacrifice, Neeko tried to talk to his father about it.

"Father, those people praying," he said as they walked along the narrow streets, "their prayers are different from the ones we say at home."

"Of course they are, son," replied his father. "That's because those people are different from us. They think that if they weep and moan about their failings, and if they watch the smoke go up from the sacrifice, God will forgive them, and give them what they ask for."

Neeko thought over what his father had said, as they continued in silence.

I will talk with Rabbi Jakov about this, he thought to himself.

"You see, we Pharisees are more careful than most people," continued his father. "We make sure that we never break the law. That way, we don't need to ask God to forgive us for anything. It's nice to go to the daily sacrifice from time to time, but for us it's just a tradition, and it's an opportunity to meet old friends. There's usually somebody to talk to. But as Pharisees, we see the sacrifices as an admission of weakness. What you are saying, when you go to the daily sacrifice for forgiveness, is, 'I'm a failure. I'm not strong enough to be good.' That's just being weak-minded.

"Remember that you are a Pharisee, my son. Don't give in to that sort of thinking. We didn't call you Nicodemus for nothing. Your name means 'ruler of the people'. We expect better things of you. You need to be strong."

Neeko said nothing in reply. He carried on walking in silence. He knew that everybody did things that upset God. He knew that he had not always behaved as he should have done.

While he had been watching those people at the sacrifice, who were calling upon God to forgive them, he had felt a strong urge to join in their prayers, but standing next to his father, he hadn't felt he could.

I wish I hadn't been born into a family of Pharisees, he thought.

CHAPTER 3

The Pilgrim Festivals

The most exciting times of year for a Jewish boy like Neeko were the Pilgrim Festivals. These were times when everybody took a holiday from work, and lots of people made their way to Jerusalem to worship God and to feast together.

Jerusalem filled with all sorts of interesting people from all over the world. Traders came from miles around to set up their stalls and sell their wares to the pilgrims. All manner of different foods could be had. The delicious smell of cooking drifted around the streets from morning until late into the evening. There would be cakes and sweets for sale, and lots of interesting stalls selling trinkets and jewellery, shoes, and clothes.

There were three main Pilgrim Festivals, and they all had their roots in things that had happened hundreds of years before in the history of the people of Israel.

Firstly, there was Passover in the springtime. This marked the beginning of the Jewish year. It was a time when people remembered how God had rescued their ancestors from a life of slavery in Egypt.

Of course, Neeko knew from his lessons with Rabbi Jakov what had happened all those years ago.

God had sent Moses to Egypt to tell the king to let all the Israelite slaves go free. The king refused. So God sent lots of dreadful plagues upon the people of Egypt – thousands of frogs, flies, and mosquitoes, locusts to eat the crops, terrible storms, and animal disease – but nothing would change the king's mind.

Finally, God sent a plague that would kill the oldest child in every family. But God made a way by which the people who trusted him could avoid such a terrible family tragedy. He gave instructions for each family to take a lamb and kill it, then paint the blood around the doorframe of their house. They were to make a meal of roast lamb, then go into the house, and stay inside until the morning.

That night the plague passed from house to house, but it passed over the houses with the blood on the doorframe. That's why this festival was called "Passover".

In the middle of the night, the king called for Moses, and told him to get out of Egypt and take all the people with him. So all the Israelite families escaped by the light of the moon. They were slaves no longer.

Every year since that time, the people of Israel have celebrated that amazing event by having a holiday, getting together with their families for a feast of roast lamb, and thanking God for rescuing them.

The next Pilgrim Festival of the year was called "the Festival of Weeks" or "Pentecost". This took place seven weeks after Passover. As Neeko knew, the Festival of Weeks celebrated the time when, after leaving Egypt, the people of Israel had arrived at a mountain called Sinai. There, Moses went up the mountain to talk with God. He came back down with some important instructions about how the people should live together as members of God's special family. These rules were given to help the people behave well and treat one another fairly.

The last Pilgrim Festival of the year was the biggest of all. It was called "the Festival of Tabernacles" or "Sukkot". Sometimes it was just called "The Feast". It was designed to remind everybody that their ancestors, the people of Israel, had for many years lived in tents. They had moved from place to place in the wild, barren country of the Sinai Desert and, despite the dry and difficult conditions, God had provided for all their needs.

This festival was a time of thanking God for the harvest of fruit, like grapes and olives, and also for water. That's why Neeko and his friends enjoyed it so much. The food was amazing.

To celebrate the Festival of Sukkot, every family built a rough shelter on their roof, or in their yard, and there they all camped for the eight days of the festival. Neeko loved this. It was great fun having everybody outside. It made it the noisiest of all the festivals.

Wherever you went in Jerusalem, during the day or even late in the evening, you could hear people talking and singing and laughing. It really was a lovely time of year.

CHAPTER 4

The Great Feast

It was during the Festival of Sukkot one year that Neeko met someone who would become a good friend for many years to come.

It was a few days before the festival was due to begin. Jerusalem was filling up with bustling crowds. Lots of families were there, and traders were beginning to set up their stalls.

The first and most important job for each family to do was to build their shelter, or "sukka", so that it would be ready for them to move into for the festival. Everywhere, people were dragging branches of trees, and carrying bundles of sticks and straw on their shoulders.

Neeko went with his father and Amoz, the family servant, out into the fields that surrounded the city. They cut branches and gathered grass and straw for their shelter. It was fun to join all the other families, laughing and calling to one another, as they collected what they needed. Neeko and his father, with the help of Amoz, tied what they had cut into bundles. Each of them carried a bundle through the narrow streets to their house, and then up the stairs to the roof, where the shelter was to be built.

Even Neeko's father seemed to be happy and more relaxed, as he began to tie sticks together to make the frame. Neeko and Amoz spent much of the day going to and from the fields, to bring back what was needed. It was great to see the shelter taking shape. Then his father began to cover the roof with grass and straw and palm leaves.

"It is important to leave some holes in the roof," said Neeko's father. "We must be able to see something of the sky, and a few stars at night."

In every odd corner, and on many of the rooftops in Jerusalem, little houses were springing up. Some were roughly built and rather scruffy. Others looked quite smart.

In a street not far from where Neeko lived was a rather grand house. Nobody lived there for most of the year, except for an old servant who kept the place swept and tidy, but at the start of every Pilgrim Festival the family moved in, so that they could be in Jerusalem and enjoy being part of the celebrations.

Having completed their own shelter, Neeko decided to have a wander round the streets to see how other people were getting on with their shelters.

The big house was arranged around a courtyard, so Neeko stood at the open gates, and peered in to see how their shelter was coming along.

"Do you need any help?" he asked the father and son, who were fixing the thatch on the roof.

The boy was just a little older than Neeko. He called in answer.

"We are running out of thatch for the roof. We shall have to make another trip to the fields."

"We have some stuff left over," replied Neeko. "Would you like some of ours?"

"That's a very kind offer," said the father. "Go with the lad, Josef, and help him bring what they can spare."

So Neeko walked back to their house, accompanied by the boy from the big house.

"I'm Josef," said the older boy, as they walked along.

"I'm Nicodemus," said Neeko. "But most people call me Neeko. Except my father of course, who always insists on calling me Nicodemus. And then there's my teacher, Rabbi Jakov. He calls me 'my boy'. I don't mind that. Rabbi Jakov is really nice, but please," added Neeko, "you can call me Neeko."

When they got to Neeko's house, his father was still up on the roof, at work on the shelter.

"This is Josef," Neeko called up to his father. "Can we give them some of the thatch that we have left over?"

Neeko's father came and leaned over the wall that surrounded the roof.

"I don't think we have any to spare," he said, scowling down at them.

"Oh, that's OK," said Josef brightly. "Don't worry. We can get some more from the fields."

Josef turned to walk back. Neeko set off with him.

"I will come and help you," he said to Josef.

"Nicodemus! Come here." His father sounded cross.

"I will have to go back," Neeko said. "I'm so sorry, Josef."

"Don't worry. It's fine. Really it is."

Neeko hurried back, and climbed up the steps to the roof.

"What is it, father?" he asked anxiously.

"Where did you meet that boy?"

"He's building a shelter not far away. They have run out of thatch, and I thought we had some to spare."

"Listen, son," said his father gruffly. "You are not to go round making friends without knowing who people are."

"I'm sorry, father," said Neeko, looking at the bundles of spare thatch piled up in the corner. "I was just trying to be helpful."

"All sorts of people come into Jerusalem at this time of year. You must remember that we are Pharisees. We must be careful whom we mix with, and what we touch. Now go and wash your hands."

Neeko went slowly and thoughtfully down to the yard. He took the special two-handled jug and went through the complex handwashing routine that he had learned from childhood.

"Sometimes," he said to himself, "I wish I hadn't been born into a family of Pharisees."

Despite the restrictions of being a Pharisee, Neeko enjoyed the festival. The food was good, and there was always singing and dancing going on in the streets.

Every morning, two processions left the Temple courts. One of them was led by the High Priest. It went out of the city by the Water Gate, and down to the pool of Siloam. The priest carried a golden jug to bring back water and pour it onto the big bronze altar during the morning sacrifice. The other procession was led by a group of Temple priests. They went to gather fresh green branches to lay down by the altar.

As a boy, Neeko had often stood with his mother to watch these processions, but this year, he wanted to be involved. His father was always a bit grumpy when it came to anything connected with the Temple, so he asked his mother if she would allow him to join one of these daily processions.

"You will have to ask your father," she said, looking at him with arms folded, and a half-smile on her face. Neeko knew what she meant, but he felt that he was big enough to challenge his father on this matter.

"Father?" he asked when he found him in the yard.

"What is it?" asked his father without looking up.

"I would like to join one of the processions tomorrow morning. I was thinking about what you said about the importance of our ancient traditions."

"Is your mother planning to accompany you?" asked his father grumpily.

"I was thinking of going on my own. Some of the boys from school will be there."

Neeko's father turned and looked at him. Neeko looked directly at his father and smiled.

"Don't worry, father. I will be good."

"Just remember that we are Pharisees, Nicodemus," said his father, returning to his ritual washing of the bowls ready for the evening meal. Neeko took that to mean "yes".

He climbed the stairs to the roof two steps at a time and joined his mother in the shelter on the roof. She was setting out the table for the evening meal. He took a fig from the dish on the table.

"Those are for later," said his mother. "What did your father say?"

"He said that I have to remember that I am a Pharisee," answered Neeko, carefully replacing the fig. "But I think it's OK to go."

Neeko thought he heard his mother whisper "Thank God," but he wasn't sure.

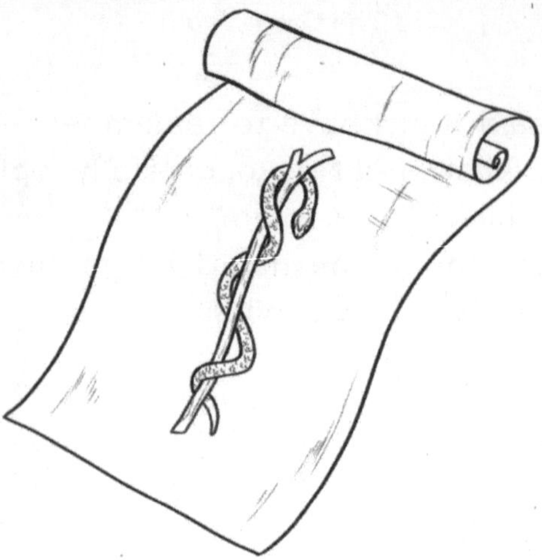

CHAPTER 5

Siloam and Back

Early the next morning, Neeko went to the pile of unused palm branches and chose a really nice one. Then, carrying the branch, he set off for the Temple courts.

Although it was still quite early, the Temple courts were full of people. Neeko was very excited to be there on his own. He wanted to join the procession that would follow the High Priest down to the pool of Siloam, to fetch water. He had stood and watched this many times as a young child, but now he was going to be a part of it.

The Temple stewards were getting everybody lined up ready for the High Priest to appear. The Temple guards were standing around, trying to keep some sort of order. Neeko joined the line next to a number of his friends from school. Already people were singing the Hallel Psalms, and swaying gently to and fro in time to the singing, as they joined the long line of people that snaked round the edges of the great Temple court.

Then a cheer went up, as the High Priest appeared. He was wearing all his robes, with the jewelled breastplate strapped to his chest. In his hands he held the golden jug, which the people saw only once a year. He raised it above his head. It sparkled and glinted in the bright morning sunshine. Everybody clapped and cheered.

Smiling broadly, he made his way to the front of the procession and joined the singers and musicians. They were all from the tribe of Levi, whose lives were dedicated to serving God at the Temple.

A great hush settled over the whole Temple court. The High Priest nodded to the leader of the singers. He was a giant of a man, with a deep, rich voice. His words echoed around the tall stone walls of the court as he began his song. Neeko was so excited. The hairs stood up on the back of his neck.

"Prai-ai-ai-se the Lo-o-o-rd," sang the leader, and all the people responded.

"Praise, O servants, you servants of the Lord."

The procession began to move, the people singing and dancing and waving branches.

"Praise the name of the Lord," sang the leader, and all the people joined in again.

> *"Let the name of the Lord be praised, both now and for evermore.*
> *From the rising of the sun in the eastern sky..."*

Many people had joined these processions year after year. They knew the routine. Everybody's branches all along the line leaned out to the left, then they all swung them high over their heads to their right as the leader sang.

"... to its going down in the west."

Then everyone waved their branches high above their heads as they sang the response at the tops of their voices.

"The name of the Lord is to be praised. Hallelujah."

So it went on, as the great procession moved out of the Temple courts, and down the narrow stepped street toward the pool of Siloam. People stood all along the route, others leaned out of their windows. They clapped and cheered, and joined in the singing. Stallholders cheered, and tossed leaves and flower petals into the air. It was so exciting for Neeko to be part of this wonderful procession of thanks and praise to God.

At last, they came to the pool of Siloam. The people in the procession gathered around as the High Priest went down the steps to the water's edge. He stood on the bottom step, as the leader began singing.

"Give thanks to the Lord, for he is good."

And all the people responded, "His love endures for ever," and waved their palm branches.

The leader looked around to see how many Roman soldiers were about. Then he sang defiantly, "Let Israel say."

The people replied with great gusto, "His love endures for ever," raising their palm branches high in the air.

Next, the leader pointed to the stewards, the singers, and the musicians.

"Let the House of Aaron say," he sang, and all those from that family line joined in the response.

"His love endures for ever."

Then the leader looked around at all the people, his face full of energy. He stretched out his arms to include the whole crowd.

"Let those who fear the Lord say."

The people responded louder than ever, waving their branches, some even dancing, as they sang.

"His love endures for ever."

It was while all this was going on that Neeko caught sight of Josef. He was among the crowd over on the other side of the pool. It was no good waving to catch his attention, because everyone was waving.

The High Priest filled the jug and lifted it high above his head. The crowd clapped and cheered as he climbed back up the steps to the pilgrim road.

With the help of the stewards, the people formed up behind the High Priest, ready for the long climb back up the pilgrim road to the Temple Mount. Neeko had lost sight of Josef among the crowd, so he just took his place in the procession.

Going back was much harder than coming down, so the singing was not so easy, and the branches were not being waved so energetically. Some of the older people were dropping back, finding that the steps were making them puff. Those with young children were leaving the procession to stand at the roadside to watch, as the rest of the crowd continued up the steadily climbing stepped street toward the Temple Mount. Neeko and the other boys managed to keep up with the main body of the procession and join in the singing.

Then, just as he was listening out for the next line from the song leader, he heard someone calling his name. He turned around to see Josef bounding up the steps of the narrow pilgrim road, waving his palm branch madly.

“Hey Josef, man. How lovely to see you,” said Neeko. Both boys were a bit out of breath with the climbing and singing. They clasped hands in greeting, then they turned and continued to follow the procession ever upwards.

“How did your shelter turn out in the end?” asked Neeko.

“It’s great,” replied Josef with a chuckle. “A bit scruffy, but hey, that’s what it’s all about after all.”

"Sorry about my dad," said Neeko. "We're Pharisees. He's a bit fussy about who we mix with."

"The Lord is good." The words drifted back from the leader of the procession. The two boys joined in the response.

"He has made his light to shine upon us. With branches in our hands we join the festive procession up to the altar." At this, the boys raised their branches above their heads.

The procession snaked its way into the Temple courts. Here the words of the singing could be heard more clearly.

"You are my God, and I will give you thanks."

"You are my God," replied the crowd, "and we will exalt you."

"Give thanks to the Lord, for he is good," sang the leader.

The two boys raised their palm branches, crossing them above their heads, and joined in the response.

"His love endures for ever." Both of them felt that theirs was going to be a lifelong friendship.

Once the procession was over, and all the stragglers had come into the court, everyone crammed together to see what they could of the morning sacrifice. They could see the smoke rising, and they could smell the wonderful rich smell of the lamb cooking. Then, as the water was poured out from the golden jug, a great cloud of white steam billowed up into the blue sky.

Everyone clapped and cheered, and those who were very thankful to their great faithful God joined in a prayer of thanks for all the fruit harvest, and his gift of water for his people. Then the Levite singers sang words from the prophet Isaiah: "With joy, we will draw water from the wells of salvation."

Neeko was watching everything that was going on around him. He could see some of the people crying real tears of joy and thanking God with sincerity. Others just stood around unmoved by all that was going on. Once again, it seemed to be clear to Neeko that some people really loved God. Whereas, for others, this was just a routine tradition.

"Are you going to come up here for the light ceremony on the last day?" asked Josef. "I will be here with my family. It's great fun."

"I will have to ask my father," said Neeko.

"I will look out for you," said Josef.

The two boys clasped hands.

"See you then," said Neeko, and he set off for home.

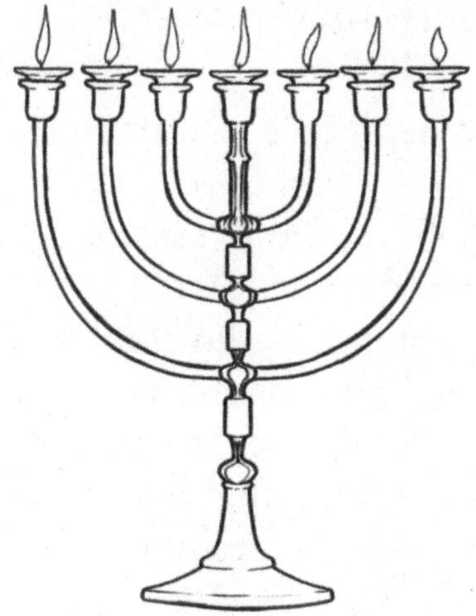

CHAPTER 6

The Last Day of the Feast

The final day of this week-long Festival of Shelters was another Sabbath, a day of rest for the people. As usual, it began at sundown on the day before, but what took place on that last day of the feast was anything but usual.

The biggest of the Temple courts was called the Court of Women. This was because both men and women were allowed to be there, whereas some of the other courts were only for men. It was in this court that four giant lampstands had been set up. They towered high above all the other Temple buildings, like four big golden trees. Each lampstand had seven branches, and on top of each branch was an enormous oil lamp. These great lampstands were so tall that they could be seen from all over

Jerusalem. Neeko could see them from the roof of his house.

As the week of the festival continued, the excitement grew. Most of the pilgrims who had come to Jerusalem for the festival wanted to be in the Temple courts for the final day. Neeko was determined to be there for the special celebrations, but he knew that his father would not want him to go. He would have to catch him when he was in a good mood.

One evening of that week, when supper was almost over, and they were still sitting round the table in their little shelter, Neeko decided to start the conversation. He looked across at his father. He had eaten well, and had drunk a few cups of wine.

"Have you seen the great lampstands in the Temple court?" Neeko began.

"Oh yes," said his mother, looking at her husband. "We used to love joining the last-day celebrations when we were young. Didn't we, darling?"

"I would love to be there this year," said Neeko.

"Hmm," said his father. "People seem to forget that it's a Sabbath day. The things that go on these days are a disgrace."

"It is the most important day of the festival," added his mother. "It's only right that people should celebrate."

"Music and dancing are hardly fitting for the Sabbath," said his father, pouring himself another cup of wine.

"I should like to see the lamps lit, and the dancing with torches," said Neeko. "Perhaps we could go as a family?"

Neeko's father choked on his wine.

"We are Pharisees, my son," he said between coughs. "God's law is sacred."

"But father, our traditions are important too. I have never been to the last-day celebrations at the Temple."

There was a long silence. Neeko sank his teeth into a fig, but he kept his eyes firmly fixed upon his father's face.

"You are almost a man, my son," said his father. "You must begin to make decisions for yourself, but don't forget. You are a Pharisee."

Neeko's mother looked across at him in the warm glow of the oil lamps. Without a word, she raised her eyebrows. Neeko understood. She had been talking to her husband.

So a few days later, as the sun began to sink and the shadows began to lengthen, signalling the beginning of the last Sabbath day of the festival, Neeko hurried toward the Temple courts. Lots of other people were going the same way, but Neeko was determined to get there before the great lamps were lit.

For strict religious Jews, and of course for Pharisees, lighting anything on the Sabbath day was considered to be work. So the Temple staff tried to make sure that the lamps were burning before the sun had completely disappeared from the western sky.

Neeko arrived in good time. The celebrations had not really started. The Temple musicians were gathering, and the men who were going to perform the fire dance with torches were standing around the brazier from which they would light their torches. The court was filling up with people, and the Temple staff were organizing them to leave a clear space for the performers. The women were being directed up the steps to the gallery above the colonnades that lined the court. They would have a grand view from up there.

Neeko looked around for Josef's family. He made his way toward the gallery steps. He knew that Josef's whole family would be there since his mother and sisters would have to go up the stairs. Then he caught sight of Josef striding toward him.

"You made it, Neeko. Well done," said Josef, reaching out to grasp Neeko's outstretched hand. "Father and I have found a great place to stand. Come and join us."

"Thank you, Josef," replied Neeko. "I desperately wanted to be here."

"You will enjoy it," said Josef. "I hope you've got your dancing shoes." Neeko went with Josef to join his father. The shadows were now stretching right across the Temple court. It was time to light the lamps.

The Levite musicians sounded a series of blasts on the ram's-horn trumpets. The crowd went silent. The celebrations were about to begin.

Starting softly at first, the flutes began to play, and the singers began the first song. Most of the people in the crowd knew the tune, and the words.

> *"I was glad, when they said to me*
> *Let us go to the house of the Lord."*

In perfect time to the music, the dancers began to move. As they danced past the brazier, they lit their torches. The troupe divided into four, and with lighted torches they danced to the four great lampstands, and circled them with a complex interweaving dance. Then they stood still and juggled with the torches, tossing them from one to another.

At some invisible signal, one dancer separated from each group and began to climb the lampstand. All of these lamplighters moved in time with each other and with the music. Each one stood against the first lamp of his lampstand. Suddenly, a torch came spinning up from the juggling dancers below. The lamplighters caught the torches and put the flames to their lamps. Tall flames leaped into the sky, while the torches went spinning down again, to be caught up in the juggling routine below.

So the spectacle continued, until all the lamps were burning brightly, lighting up the whole Temple court. The last lamps to be lit were the middle ones on each lampstand. The lamplighters stood against the central unlit lamp, their costumes sparkling in the light of the flames. It was as if they were part of the decorations. Then spinning up from the dancers below came another torch, and the last of the lamps were lit.

Everybody clapped, and the trumpets sounded. The music continued, and the people sang:

"And now our feet are standing,
Standing within your courts
O Jerusalem."

The lamplighters came back down, and joined the rest of the dancers. The four groups came together again. The music changed, and the dancers began a complex dance in the middle of the court, while juggling with their torches. It was a dazzling performance. Neeko was amazed. He stood there with eyes wide. He had never seen anything like this before.

Young girls, with flowers in their hair, moved through the crowd carrying baskets of fruit and nuts and sweetmeats. Neeko was so absorbed with the fire dance that he didn't take anything when a basket came past, and the girl passed him by. Josef took a handful of roasted almonds.

"Come on, Neeko. Join the celebration," he said, passing him a few nuts. "These are for you."

“Thanks, Josef,” said Neeko as he took the nuts. “This is all so amazing.”

“It will be time to dance soon,” said Josef. “I hope you are going to join in.”

“You will have to show me the steps,” replied Neeko with a smile. “I’ve not done much dancing.”

“It’s easy,” replied Josef. “You just move with the music, and go with the flow.”

After the dancers with the torches had finished their display, other dancers took their place in the middle of the court. These were girls in long white dresses, with leaves, flowers, and jewels woven into their braided hair. The light from the great lamps high above them sparkled in their jewelled headdresses, and set the shadows dancing beneath their feet.

The music for these dances was a melody to a familiar song, slow and gentle. It stirred Neeko deeply. The people standing around the edge of the court, and the women on the balconies, began to join in the singing.

The words were from the same Psalm as before:

“Pray for the peace of Jerusalem.
May those who love you be secure.
May there be peace within your walls,
And safety within your towers.”

The dancers divided into smaller groups, and then divided again, until each girl was dancing alone. They each danced out toward the crowd and, taking a hand, led the people into the middle of the court. Before long, the whole court was alive with dancing and singing.

Neeko, Josef, and his father all joined the dancing. They sang the well-known words, as they linked their arms:

> *"For the sake of my brothers and friends,*
> *I will say 'Peace be within you.'*
> *For the sake of the Lord our God*
> *I will seek your prosperity."*

The dancing and singing continued long into the night. Some of the dances were beautifully performed by proper dancers, while everyone else stood and watched and clapped in time to the music. Other dances were for everybody to join, whether they were any good at dancing or not. Nobody seemed to mind if Neeko turned the wrong way, or got in a muddle with his feet.

Neeko had never enjoyed such a night before. High above their heads, the great flames from the lampstands joined in the dancing, as they leaped up into the night sky.

All too soon, a faint glow began to appear in the eastern sky. Dawn was approaching. At this point, the music changed. Most people knew what to do. They linked arms to form many circles of dancers right across the Temple court. The circles turned first one way, and then the other, as everybody sang:

"How good and pleasant it is,
When brothers live together in harmony.
It is like the precious oil
Poured upon the head
Running down upon the beard
Running down on Aaron's beard
Running down upon the collar of his robe.
It is as if the very dew of Mount Hermon
Was falling on Mount Zion.
For there the Lord pours out his blessing.
For there the Lord pours out his blessing.
For there the Lord pours out his blessing.
Even life for evermore,
For evermore,
For ever, ever, more."

Then the trumpeters from the Levite musicians appeared on top of the two towers that stood above the gate to the inner Temple courts. They put their silver trumpets to their lips, and sounded a fanfare that could be heard above the noise of singing and dancing. In fact, it could be heard all over the city of Jerusalem. It signalled the end of the night's celebrations.

Everybody clapped and cheered, and began to wish one another God's peace – "Shalom" – as they prepared to leave the Temple courts.

This last and greatest day of the festival was a time when many new friendships were forged, and here the friendship between Neeko and Josef was cemented. Together with Josef's father, the two boys went to wait for Josef's mother and sisters as they came down the gallery steps. Then, together, they walked back to their homes with arms linked, singing all the way.

At the door of Josef's house, they stood together.

"We will be returning to our home in Arimathea tomorrow," said Josef. "But we will be back as usual for Passover in the spring."

"Let's make a point of getting together again then," said Neeko. "Thanks for your company. I really have enjoyed this night so much."

The two boys clasped hands above their heads.

"Brothers for ever," said Josef.

"Shalom," said Neeko, and he gave Josef a friendly punch, before turning and walking back home to a chorus of "Shalom" from Josef's family.

CHAPTER 7

John Spots a Snakes' Nest

As the years rolled by, Neeko and Josef spent time together at most of the Pilgrim Festivals in Jerusalem.

Josef's family were very wealthy. His father knew a lot about metals and how they were mined and refined. As Josef grew into manhood, he learned the business from his father. They journeyed together to many distant places. Then as his father grew older, and not so strong, Josef took over the business.

Because he was rich, he knew a lot of important people, including Romans, so Josef was invited to be part of the Jewish council in Jerusalem.

Neeko, on the other hand, loved to study the Hebrew Scriptures. He was very clever, so as he grew older, he became a teacher himself. People came to him for advice, especially about legal matters and family disputes. He became widely respected for his wise judgments over how to interpret the Scriptures, and other traditional writings by rabbis from the past. So Neeko, too, was invited to be a member of the big religious council in Jerusalem.

This council was called the Sanhedrin. It was made up of seventy-one men, who made it their business to oversee the religious life of the Jewish people, and try to keep the Romans happy. The High Priest from the Temple was in charge of the Sanhedrin. The place where they met was called "The Hall of Hewn Stones". The council members sat around the edge of this hall, with a large stone-paved floor in the middle. It made their voices sound loud and echoey and rather important.

Some council members belonged to particular family groups, or religious sects. This meant that sometimes the arguments became rather heated. When that happened, the Hall of Hewn Stones was a very noisy place indeed.

Everybody in Jerusalem was talking about a long-haired preacher, who was attracting crowds down by the Jordan river. His name was John. He was helping people to see where they were behaving badly, and baptizing them in the river if they chose to change their ways.

When the subject of John came up in the Sanhedrin council, the conversation grew noisier and noisier. Some people thought he was a good man, others thought he was a troublemaker.

"Why didn't he come and ask this council's permission before he started all this rumpus?" asked one member.

"He's attracting a lot of people," said another. "The Romans won't take kindly to that. They don't like crowds."

"Some of us will remember his father from years ago," added the High Priest. "He was a good and godly man, but wild and rebellious sons are not uncommon these days."

"I think," said Neeko, standing up, "that we should go down to the Jordan, and hear what this John fellow has to say. It's hardly possible for us to make any sort of judgment, when we have never heard him for ourselves."

For once, there was general agreement among the members of the council. It was decided that as many of them as possible should take a few days off and visit the Jordan preacher.

It was a good long day's walk from Jerusalem to the Jordan, so when Neeko and his good friend Josef set out early one morning, they took food and water for their journey. They planned to stay overnight at an inn on their way there, and on their way back. The visit would take three days altogether.

As they left Jerusalem, they were surprised to see how many other people were on the move down toward Jericho, and to the Jordan beyond.

"It's like going up to Jerusalem for one of the Pilgrim Festivals," said Josef, "except that everyone's going in the opposite direction."

When they stopped at the inn on the way, it was very busy.

"Good old John," said the innkeeper, as he welcomed them and found them a place to sleep. "He's bringing us plenty of business. We are usually quiet at this time of year."

The following morning, Neeko and Josef set off early, before the sun was too hot, and followed the growing trail of people down to the Jordan river. It was not difficult to find John. There was an enormous crowd gathered on the bank of the river, at the spot where he was preaching and baptizing. They could hear John's voice ringing out loud and clear above the noise of the crowd.

"I know that some of you think that I am the Messiah. I have heard that talk, but no, I am not. I will say it again. I am not the Messiah. I am the one of whom the prophet speaks:

"'A voice is crying in the wilderness. Prepare the way of the Lord.'"

At this, the crowd clapped and cheered.

Neeko could see that a number of his fellow Pharisees from the Sanhedrin council were there. They stood out from the crowd, with their striped prayer-scarves and their grim faces. Neeko felt out of place among this great crowd, who were enjoying every moment of John's preaching. He and Josef stood on their own, away from the rest of the council members. Neeko wanted to pull off his scarf and tuck it away out of sight, but by now he was a rabbi himself, and a respected teacher of Jewish law. He knew that if any of the council members saw him without his prayer-scarf, there would be questions to answer.

Suddenly, John looked up, and scanned the crowd standing above him on the riverbank.

"Hello," he said, pretending to count all the council members with his outstretched finger. "What have we here? A proper little nest of poisonous snakes. What brings you here, eh?"

The council members looked at one another and fidgeted uncomfortably. The people in the crowd were fascinated. Many were smiling. Nobody would dare to speak to a member of the Sanhedrin in this way, but John didn't seem to care. Neeko tried to stand out of sight. He felt that John was looking right into his heart.

"It's no use saying to yourselves, 'We can trace our ancestors back to Abraham, so we will be alright.' You need to show, by what you do, that you really want to change your ways. Didn't you know that trees that produce no fruit get chopped down, and thrown on the fire?

"For those of you who want to put your lives right with God, I will baptize with water, but there is someone coming after me, who is far more powerful than I am. He will baptize you with fire, and the Holy Spirit. He will be like a farmer sorting out his grain at harvest time. Wheat in one pile," said John, seeming to point at particular people in the crowd, "and chaff in the other, ready to burn up in God's fire."

As Neeko watched, he saw one person after another walk down into the water, talk quietly with John for a while, and then let him baptize them in the river. Each one came up dripping from the river, to find their place again among the crowd while everybody clapped and cheered.

Neeko was deeply moved by what he saw and heard. He knew that the Pharisees really were a nest of poisonous snakes, infecting the people with their twisted teaching and self-interest. There were things in his own life that he was ashamed of too. He would really like to show that he was sorry.

"What do you think?" he asked, turning to Josef.

"It's the truth, Neeko," replied Josef. "Uncomfortable, but true." The two men stood out of sight behind the crowd.

"You know what, Josef?" continued Neeko. "I think I could go down into the water with this prophet John. I know there are things in my life that need straightening out."

"Steady on, Neeko," replied Josef. "I know what you mean, but not with all these people watching. There are some council members here today. I think it would be wise to wait for another opportunity."

"Maybe," replied Neeko, but his attention was again focused on John as the preaching continued. Neeko was fascinated by this man and what he was doing. This baptism was so different from the sort of washing that he was accustomed to. These people were not trying to get rid of the dirt from the outside of their bodies. They were not trying to wash off contamination from people they considered to be "unclean", like the Pharisees did. They were dealing with things that were wrong in their own lives. They were facing the evil that was on the inside, the sin in their own hearts.

If only I hadn't been born into a family of Pharisees, thought Neeko. *I would be straight down there, and into the Jordan with John.*

Later that day, Neeko and Josef walked slowly and thoughtfully back to the inn, where they had stayed the night before.

"If John really is that voice crying in the wilderness," said Josef, "then perhaps we will see God's promised Messiah during our lifetime."

"Some think he's already here," replied Neeko. "I was talking to a man standing next to me in the crowd, who has been coming to hear John for some time. He says that John has met the Messiah. He calls him 'God's Lamb'."

"God's Lamb, eh? Now that is interesting," said Josef thoughtfully.

"Yes," replied Neeko. "God's Lamb who will somehow be like a sacrifice to take away all the sins of the world."

"Really?" exclaimed Josef. "You Pharisees are not going to be very comfortable with that."

Neeko glanced at his friend, as they walked along side by side.

"You know, Josef," he said, "I sometimes wish I hadn't been born into a family of Pharisees."

"Don't let anyone else hear you say that," said Josef, looking at Neeko. "You are supposed to be one of our leading teachers."

"I know that," replied Neeko, "but I feel trapped by all these petty rules and religious rituals that we are supposed to practise. I have a feeling that it doesn't please God as much as some people think it does."

They walked along in silence for a while, each man absorbed in his own thoughts. The sun was beginning to sink toward the western horizon, their shadows growing longer as they danced along behind them on the dusty road.

At last, they could see in the distance the little cluster of buildings to where they were heading.

"I should like to meet this 'Lamb'," said Neeko solemnly.

"I'm ready for supper, if that's what you mean," said Josef with a chuckle. His comment broke the spell of their serious discussion. Both men were laughing as they turned into the yard of the inn.

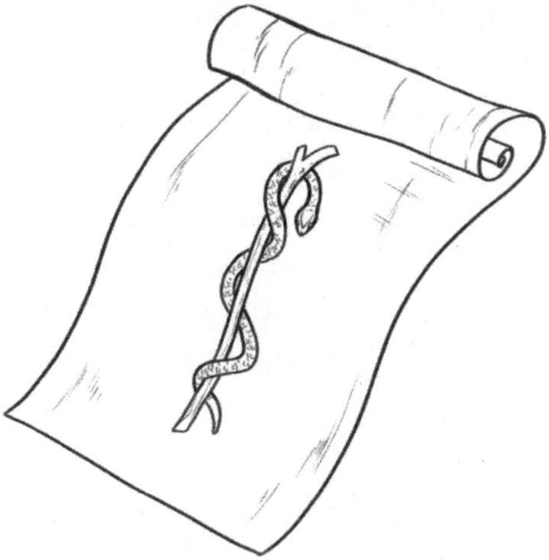

CHAPTER 8

Jesus from Nazareth

It was not many months after Neeko and Josef's visit to John at the Jordan that news reached the council in Jerusalem. John had been arrested by Herod, and locked away in his fortress stronghold at Machaerus.

But other news was coming from Galilee. A man called Jesus, who came from Nazareth, was preaching and teaching in the towns and villages that lined the shores of Lake Galilee. There were reports of miracles. Large crowds had been gathering to hear this man's teaching. Once again, many of the council members were troubled by what they were hearing. So they sent a small group of spies to bring back a report.

When the spies returned, the Sanhedrin council gathered in their usual place. Neeko took his seat next to Josef. He was particularly eager to hear news of this man Jesus, who was causing even more of a stir than John ever had.

The spies stood in the middle of the paved area, while the council members sat around the edge of the hall. Everyone was chatting, so there was already a lot of noise.

After a while, the High Priest stood, and held up his hand. The council went quiet.

"Gentlemen," he began. "As you are all aware, we have received news of a rabbi, who is attracting crowds in Galilee. We have commissioned these men before us today to visit the area, and make an assessment of the situation on our behalf." He nodded to the spies, and then sat down. The leader of the spies stepped forward, and began.

"Respected rulers, teachers, members of the Sanhedrin, as requested, we have been to the region of Galilee, where Rabbi Jesus is at work. For some days, we have joined the crowds that have gathered to hear this prophet's teaching. And to observe the miracles that he is performing."

"We have seen blind people receive their sight, and deaf people their hearing," said one of the other spies.

"People who have been unable to walk for years have been healed," said another. "They just picked up their sleeping-mats and walked away."

"It is all truly remarkable," said the leader. "Even lepers are made clean."

All three men were getting more and more animated, as they reported all that they had seen. Their voices grew louder. Their hands became more active.

"Then there is the teaching. It is simple and clear, so that even a child could understand it."

"He is truly a remarkable man. People are hanging upon his every word and calling him a great rabbi."

"He speaks with considerable authority."

"Yes, indeed," added the leader. "Many of the people are saying that he speaks with greater authority than..." Here the spy's voice tailed away. He was going to say "than the scribes and Pharisees", but he suddenly realized that this council was full of them. He coughed noisily, and stumbled over his next few words.

"... er, greater authority than anything, than anything that anyone had, er, ever heard before."

Caiaphas, the High Priest, was listening intently. His arms were folded. His face like thunder.

"The council has paid you good money to undertake an investigation on our behalf," he growled. "It sounds to me as if you have been taken in by this imposter."

The leader of the spies stepped forward once more, and addressed the council in a more measured way.

"Sir," he said, turning to the High Priest, "and gentlemen of the Sanhedrin. Please do not think that we have been deceived, or led astray by some showman or trickster. We have carried out our investigations thoroughly, and with great care. We have spoken to some of his close followers, and to many of the local people, who have been listening to his teaching and witnessing the miracles that have taken place. We are in no doubt that we have seen extraordinary events, and what we have heard is truly exceptional.

"If we have seemed to be overexcited or emotional in our response, it is simply that we have seen and heard things that are beyond our normal experience."

Neeko turned to Josef and whispered, "We must find a way of meeting this man Jesus. I would love to have a chance to speak with him in private."

"You are right," replied Josef. "Perhaps he will be in Jerusalem for the Passover festival."

"Let's hope so," said Neeko, turning his attention back to the men standing before them. There were questions that he wanted to ask, but he wasn't going to do so here, in front of the Sanhedrin council. Clearly, these men had been deeply moved by what they had seen and heard.

"Could this man Jesus," Neeko asked himself, "be the 'Lamb' that John talked about?"

He made up his mind to try to find a way of meeting one of these spies somewhere quiet, for a private chat.

CHAPTER 9

Secret Meeting

Having spoken privately to one of the men who had been sent to Galilee as spies for the Sanhedrin, Neeko was determined to find a way of meeting Jesus himself. Passover was approaching, so Neeko hoped that Jesus might come to Jerusalem for the festival.

The inns and lodging houses started to get busy. Families were arriving to set up camp in the fields around the city. Traders were setting up their stalls. There were more people in the streets, more noise, more music, more delicious smells. There was no mistaking that Jerusalem was building up for the Pilgrim Festival of Passover.

He had always loved the Pilgrim Festivals but, as Neeko grew older, it was Passover that was becoming increasingly important to him. As a boy, he had liked to watch as all the Passover lambs were brought into the city from the surrounding countryside. They always arrived some days before the festivities began. To him, the noise and smell of all those sheep, jostling their way through the narrow streets, heralded the countdown to Passover.

Since he had grown into manhood, Neeko had seldom gone to watch the sheep arriving, but this year was different. Having heard John talk about God's Lamb who would take away the evil in the world, something had been at work in Neeko's heart and mind.

Perhaps the Pharisees were wrong. They thought they were without sin, but he knew that among his fellow Pharisees there was plenty to be ashamed of. He knew that in his own life, he had made mistakes. He was by no means perfect.

Thoughtfully, he wandered down to the Sheep Gate, and stood there, just as he had done as a boy. He watched the rough shepherds from the pastures around Bethlehem bringing their flocks of lambs into the city in time for the Passover celebrations. He wondered whether Jesus would come up to Jerusalem to celebrate the Passover festival. If he did, Neeko was determined to meet him.

As things turned out, he didn't have to search too hard to find him. The following day, when

Neeko took his seat among the councillors of the Sanhedrin, everyone was talking about Jesus from Nazareth.

"What's been going on?" he asked Josef.

"There's been a rumpus in the Temple courts," replied Josef. "Rabbi Jesus has made a bit of a stir. Yesterday, he went into the courts where all the trading goes on. He had a piece of rope in his hand. He drove all the animals out, and turned over the tables where they do the money-changing. He was quite impressive, by all accounts."

"Wow!" exclaimed Neeko. "I wish I could have been there."

"The money went all over the floor. The dealers were scrabbling around on their hands and knees trying to pick it all up, and arguing about which coins were whose. Jesus told them in no uncertain terms, 'Don't you know that this is supposed to be a place for prayer? You have made it into a den of robbers.'"

"Good for him," responded Neeko. "That needed saying. The High Priest should have taken action years ago, but we all know there's money to be made from having the traders there."

The business in the Hall of Hewn Stones that day was very noisy. It was all about this new rabbi who had turned up in Jerusalem, and what should be done about him. Neeko and Josef kept quiet, but Neeko was more determined than ever to find a way of meeting with him secretly.

Neeko was eager to have a private conversation with Jesus, but it was proving difficult to do so. Whenever he was in public, Jesus was surrounded by crowds of people. Neeko's only chance would be to find out where Jesus was staying, and meet him there.

He decided to make his visit after sundown, so that nobody would see him arrive or leave. He knew that his fellow Pharisees were suspicious of Jesus. They considered him to be a troublemaker. Neeko knew that some of the members of the council were ruthless men. They would stop at nothing. He would have to be careful.

Once Neeko had discovered where Jesus and a few of his close disciples were staying, he settled upon a particular evening during the festival week to make his visit.

Normally, Neeko would have taken his servant with him when walking the streets of Jerusalem after dark, but during the festival the streets were well lit, with torches set in iron brackets along the walls. The traders' stalls were open for business. He knew that it would be pretty safe to go alone.

He threw his heavy winter cloak over his shoulders. It had a hood that he could pull over his head when necessary. He lit a lantern. The Romans didn't like people moving about after dark without carrying a light. He didn't want to draw attention to himself.

So he set out, walking briskly, but keeping to the shadows.

"I feel like a street criminal," he said to himself, "avoiding the light like this." But the streets were still busy with people. Nobody took any notice of him.

He arrived at the house and knocked on the door. After a few moments he heard footsteps inside, then a voice.

"Who is it?"

"My name is Nicodemus," said Neeko. "I have come to talk with Jesus from Nazareth. I believe he is staying here."

"Wait one moment," said the voice, and Neeko could hear footsteps and muffled voices from within the house.

After a few moments, the door was opened by the house servant.

"Come on in. He's expecting you," he said.

That's odd, thought Neeko. He stepped inside and slipped off his sandals. He blew out the lamp in his lantern and set it down by his shoes.

"I will take you up," said the servant.

"I really want to speak to him alone, if that's possible," said Neeko.

"OK. Follow me," said the servant, setting off up a flight of rough wooden stairs, the light of his lamp casting great dark shadows on the wall as he climbed. Neeko followed him.

At the top he could see an open door. Lamplight was spilling out onto the boarded floor.

"He is through there," said the servant.

"Come on in," said a voice. "Come on in, and welcome."

Cautiously, Neeko slipped through the door. He wasn't sure what to expect. A man was sitting at a lighted table. He stood up and came toward Neeko with arms stretched out in welcome.

"You must be Neeko," said Jesus warmly. "I have been looking forward to meeting you." Neeko was surprised to hear him using his familiar name.

"I wanted to speak with you alone, if that's possible," said Neeko. "It's rather personal."

Jesus gestured towards the bench by the table.

"Please, make yourself comfortable," said Jesus, nodding to the servant, who left the room and closed the door behind him. Neeko sat on the bench opposite Jesus. He slipped off his cloak and carefully folded it onto the bench next to him. It gave him time to gather his thoughts. Jesus poured two cups of water.

"Now, tell me," said Jesus, pushing a cup toward him and moving a bowl of dates to within his reach. "What is troubling you? Something is on your mind, I think."

Neeko took a sip of water. He was very used to meeting people, and discussing difficult matters with them, but here, alone with Jesus, he felt strangely nervous.

"Er, teacher?" he began hesitantly. "Everybody knows that you have been sent by God. No one could do the miracles that you are doing unless God was with him."

Jesus looked intently at Neeko.

This man can see everything, thought Neeko. *He knows exactly what I am thinking.*

"What you need is a completely new start," said Jesus. "You will have to be born all over again to be part of God's Kingdom. You won't even be able to catch a glimpse of it otherwise."

Time and time again throughout his life, Neeko had wished that he could make a clean new start. He had wished that he hadn't been born into a family of Pharisees. Perhaps Jesus knew how he felt.

"Is there really a way that this can happen for a man of my age?" he asked. "I can't go back inside my mother and be born a second time, now can I? That's impossible."

"I'm not talking about natural birth," replied Jesus. "Even if you were able to be born a second time in that way, it would only make a difference to your natural body. No, to be changed in a deeper way, you will have to be born by God's Spirit."

That makes sense, thought Neeko. *I think I can follow that.*

"When you see God's Spirit at work, it's like watching the wind blowing things along. You can't see the wind, but you can see what it's doing. That's what it's like to be made new by God's Spirit."

"That's remarkable. How can this happen for me?"

"I have to say that I find it a bit odd having to explain things like this to you," said Jesus with a warm smile. "You are a respected teacher in Israel, and yet you seem to have little knowledge of such important matters as these.

"We have seen God's Spirit do some amazing things in people's lives, yet it is the teachers and leaders like you, Neeko, who refuse to believe the reports. If you can't believe the things that God has done among the ordinary people around you, how are you going to believe if I tell you of the wonders of Heaven?"

Neeko knew that what he was hearing was the truth. He buried his face in his hands, and heaved a great sigh.

"I am no stranger to Heaven," whispered Jesus. "I might be called 'Son of Man', but Heaven is where I am from, you know. One day, this body of mine will be lifted up high, for everyone to see. I am sure you will remember, Neeko, how Moses set up a bronze snake on a pole in the desert in full view of the people. Those who had been bitten by the snakes could look in faith at that bronze snake, and be healed from their poisonous snakebite. In a similar way, those who look to me in faith will gain a new heavenly life that is eternal."

Neeko was still sitting with his elbows on the table, his face in his hands. Memories of those early days in the schoolroom came flooding back into his mind. He remembered copying out the story of the snake on the pole, letter by letter. He could smell the cakes baking in Mrs Jakov's kitchen. He could hear the voice of dear old Rabbi Jakov.

"Remember boys, God is always looking for people who will trust him."

There were tears in Neeko's eyes as he lifted his head and looked again into the earnest gaze of this young rabbi from Nazareth.

"This is how much God loved the world," said Jesus. "He gave his Son, his one and only Son. If you will trust him, Neeko, you will not be lost. You will begin a new life as a child in God's heavenly Kingdom."

Neeko looked at Jesus. He was not able to speak. He just nodded in agreement.

"You must understand," continued Jesus, "that my Father didn't send me into the world to find fault with everybody. Not at all. I have come to save them. God will not judge the people who believe in his Son. It's the ones who reject him who will be in trouble." Neeko nodded again.

"In these days, God has sent his light into the world." Jesus looked directly into Neeko's eyes. "But some people prefer to stay in the shadows."

Neeko remembered his walk through the streets that evening, the hood of his big winter cloak pulled over his face. He took a sip of water. It gave him something to do, and an excuse to turn his eyes away from the direct gaze of Jesus.

He was not used to this kind of talk – simple, direct, and personal. Somehow, this man Jesus seemed to be able to connect with things in his own experience. Neeko was much more comfortable with complicated arguments about the Hebrew Scriptures or Jewish tradition. He could compare the opinions of one rabbi against another. He could take the Hebrew language to pieces, and put it all back together again, but this Jesus was not like any rabbi that he had met before. He spoke with clear language that even a child could understand, but he spoke with such strength and love and authority. It was terrifying. It was too much for Neeko.

"I am going to have to leave," said Neeko, getting up from the table. "You have given me a lot to think about."

"Well then, Neeko," said Jesus gently, getting up and holding the door open. "I hope we will have the opportunity to meet again. There is so much more to talk about."

Neeko set off down the stairs, and then realized that he had left his cloak behind. He turned around to find that Jesus was standing at the top of the stairs. He was smiling. The cloak was in his hand.

"Thank you," said Neeko, taking the coat and returning down the stairs. At the bottom, he wriggled his feet back into his sandals, and lifted the latch on the house door to leave.

"Don't forget your lantern, sir," said the servant. "Here, let me light it for you." He lit a taper from the lamp on the wall and set the lantern glowing merrily.

"Will we be seeing you again, sir?" he asked, handing the lantern to Neeko.

"Perhaps," replied Neeko as he took the lantern. "I don't really know. He's given me a lot to think about." And with that, he stepped out into the dark street.

He walked home briskly. There was still a lot going on in the streets, but Neeko's mind was elsewhere. He was working through everything that Jesus had said.

When he arrived home, he quietly opened the door and went in. His servant, Amoz, could see that he had been crying.

"Is there anything the matter, sir?" Amoz asked.

"No," said Neeko, reaching for the bag that hung from his belt.

"Here," he said, handing his servant a few silver coins. "Go and have a walk in the streets. There is still plenty going on. I need to be quiet for a while."

"Very good, sir," said the faithful old family servant. "I can see you need a bit of peace and quiet. I will take your lantern with me, sir." He took his coat and stepped out into the night, softly closing the door behind him.

Neeko sat down at the table. He buried his face in his hands and wept.

"Why didn't I stay longer?" he sobbed. "If only I could be born into a new way of life. That is what I have always wanted. O Lord, have mercy on me."

Neeko stayed like this for a long time. As he wept, he felt the old Pharisee dissolving away from inside. Something new was beginning in his heart. He raised his head and leaned back in his chair. The lamp on the table burned brightly, the flame stretching up to a tall, sharp point. As he watched, it wavered and bent in the draught from the ill-fitting window-shutter. He remembered Jesus' words.

"When you see God's Spirit at work, it's like watching the wind blowing things along."

"Spirit of God," prayed Neeko, "blow through me. I want to be born anew into your eternal Kingdom."

Suddenly, the flame dipped and flickered. It almost went right out, but it soon recovered and burned brightly again. Neeko could feel a draught, but it was only Amoz returning from the street. Neeko smiled.

"Thank you, Lord," he whispered.

"You are looking better, sir," said his servant.

"You are back quickly," replied Neeko. "I thought you would take the opportunity to have a relaxing evening, buy a few things, and have a chat with some friends."

"I have done all of that, sir," said Amoz, "but it's getting late."

"Is it really?" said Neeko. "I have been sitting here longer than I thought."

"Perhaps sir, but I have brought you some lovely spiced cakes."

"I can smell them," said Neeko. "They remind me of the cakes old Rabbi Jakov's wife used to make for us when we had finished our lessons."

Amoz unwrapped the cakes and put them into a small basket on the table.

"They are still warm, sir," he said, looking at Neeko with a smile.

Neeko took the basket and held it under his nose. He drew in a long breath of the spicy fragrance.

"This brings it all back," he said. "That old schoolroom next to the synagogue, and dear old Rabbi Jakov."

"Yes sir, I remember taking you there when you were small."

"This evening, Amoz," said Neeko, looking directly at his old servant, "I have met another rabbi. He is so much wiser, and more gracious than even old Rabbi Jakov. And I have learned a very important lesson. So, I think I am ready for one of these spiced cakes."

CHAPTER 10

Poisonous Snakes

Over the next few years, reports were filtering through to Jerusalem from Galilee about Jesus, his preaching, and the many miracles that he was doing. He visited Jerusalem a number of times, and he constantly found himself at odds with the Jewish religious leaders. They didn't like him, so they called him "Jesus from Nazareth", because most people despised the town of Nazareth.

As members of the Sanhedrin council, Neeko and Josef often found themselves in disagreement with other members of the council, especially when the subject of Jesus came up in their discussions.

On a number of occasions, the council had talked about arresting Jesus. They wanted to stone him to death, but it hadn't been possible, because there were always too many people around him.

On one occasion, while Jesus was teaching the people in the Temple courts, the council sent a squad of Temple guards to arrest him and bring him back for questioning.

After some time, the guards came back. They stood empty-handed on the stone floor in front of the council.

"Well, where is he?" asked the High Priest. "Why haven't you brought him in?"

"We went to get him. He was in the Temple courts, surrounded by crowds of people," said one of the guards.

"We listened to what he was saying, and it all made perfectly good sense," said another. "We have never heard anyone speaking like he does."

"What you mean," shouted one of the leading Pharisees, "is that he has deceived you too! Has anyone on this council believed in him, eh?"

One of the guards shrugged. The Pharisee pointed at him accusingly.

"No, they haven't," he shouted. "Only that crowd of ignorant people who follow him like so many sheep. What do they know about the Law? They are cursed, the lot of them."

As this conversation became more heated, Neeko felt that he should say something. He stood up.

"Brothers," he began, "I must appeal to you, to deal with this matter with wisdom." He looked around at the angry faces of the council, and then at the Temple guards standing in front of them, fidgeting uncomfortably.

"Does our law condemn a man without giving him a proper hearing? We need more information before we can act."

"Where did you come from, Nicodemus?" shouted the same Pharisee rudely. "Maybe you are from Galilee too, eh?" Some of the council members laughed. "I thought you were supposed to be a great teacher of the law," continued the Pharisee venomously. "Look into it. God's Messiah is not going to come out of Galilee."

This stinging attack hurt Neeko. He could have defended himself, by quoting some words from the great prophet Isaiah, but he decided to say nothing. He just sat down.

He was beginning to realize that the tension between him and the Sanhedrin was reaching breaking point. He felt that he could not hold out much longer, pretending to be a good Pharisee. He knew that deep down, he wanted to be free of it all. He wanted to rid himself of all these false religious practices. He wanted to pursue the truth. He wanted to follow Jesus.

Then news came from the nearby village of Bethany that shook the Sanhedrin council.

CHAPTER 11

The Plot to Kill Jesus

An amazing miracle had taken place in Bethany, just a few miles along the road from Jerusalem. For the Sanhedrin council, this was too close for comfort, and it made them more determined than ever to silence Jesus.

In Bethany, Jesus had some very close friends. They were two sisters and a brother. Their names were Martha, Mary, and Lazarus.

One day, Lazarus fell seriously ill. The sisters sent an urgent message to Jesus, but he didn't turn up, and so Lazarus died. The body was wrapped up in grave clothes and laid in a stone tomb. A great, heavy circular rock was rolled over the opening to close it off.

Four days later, Jesus arrived in Bethany with his disciples. He found the sisters in tears.

"Where on earth have you been?" asked Martha accusingly. "If you had got here earlier, my brother would not have died."

"Don't worry, Martha," answered Jesus calmly. "Resurrection and life are what I am about."

Martha and Mary took him along the road to the graveyard. All the mourners and relatives followed. They thought that Jesus was going to do the polite thing, and weep at the tomb.

When they got there, everyone was crying. Jesus was so touched by their pain that he couldn't help crying too. But then he told them to do a crazy thing.

"Take the stone away from the door," he said.

"But Lord," said Martha, "our brother has been dead for days. You can't go in there. The smell will be disgusting."

"If you believe," answered Jesus, "you will see God do an amazing thing."

The big stone was rolled back from the door of the tomb, and wedged in place. Jesus looked up to Heaven, and prayed.

"Father, thank you for hearing me," he said. "I know you always hear me, but I want these people to know that it is really you who has sent me to them."

Everyone was listening intently, straining to hear Jesus' words. Then they heard him take a deep breath. They thought he was about to start sobbing, but no. He surprised them all, with a loud and powerful command.

"Lazarus, come out of there!" All the people were shocked. They stood in silence, watching and listening. No one dared to speak.

A faint sound of movement came from inside the tomb. It sounded like someone fumbling and shuffling. Then, out through the rough-hewn doorway Lazarus appeared, wrapped from head to toe in linen grave-wrappings, his face covered with a cloth.

"Unwrap him, someone," said Jesus with a smile. "We can't send him home like that."

The people watched in amazement as the live body of Lazarus was unwrapped. The linen wrappings were still sticky with embalming ointment.

Many of the local mourners who saw these wonderful things believed in Jesus, but there were some in the crowd who were there to cause trouble. They had come specially from Jerusalem to see what Jesus was getting up to. Immediately, they slipped away from the crowd and hurried back to Jerusalem, to tell the council what Jesus had done.

So it was that a special meeting of the Sanhedrin was called. Neeko and Josef took their seats. One of the chief priests stood up and addressed the meeting.

"Gentlemen, brothers," he began. "You have probably heard what this Jesus fellow has been up to in Bethany. He is performing what look like remarkable miracles, and the people are being taken in. If this sort of thing continues, there will be hundreds of people following him. The Romans will be unsettled and are likely to respond with force. We will lose our Temple. In fact, our very nation is at risk."

Then Caiaphas, the High Priest, stood up. He looked strangely calm.

"Brothers, we need to understand what is going on here. I feel that it would be better for this one man to die, than for the whole nation to be destroyed."

Neeko looked at Josef. Josef raised his eyebrows, but said nothing. The council continued their discussions. They were trying to work out a way of getting rid of Jesus. They concluded that, as it would soon be Passover, they would arrest Jesus when he came to Jerusalem for the festival.

"If anyone can find out where he is staying," said the High Priest, "it is important that they inform this council. We cannot take him in public. There will be a riot, then we will all be in real trouble."

After the council meeting, Neeko and Josef walked slowly and thoughtfully back to their homes.

"Anyone would think that bringing someone back to life was a crime," said Josef.

"Things are getting nasty," replied Neeko. "I think we are going to find ourselves in a very difficult position."

"It is a sad day, when what is so good is called evil, by those who think they are good," said Josef.

"And when those who are supposed to teach people what is right, conspire to do such evil things," said Neeko.

"John was right," said Josef. "They really are a nest of poisonous snakes."

"I remember Jesus saying to me that night," said Neeko, "that God has sent his light into the world, but we prefer darkness, because what we do is so evil."

"It's true for all of us," said Josef. "We have all been bitten by the poisonous snake."

The two men continued walking in silence.

"Passover is fast approaching," said Neeko, "but I am not feeling the usual excitement."

"I know what you mean," said Josef. "Things are looking rather bleak."

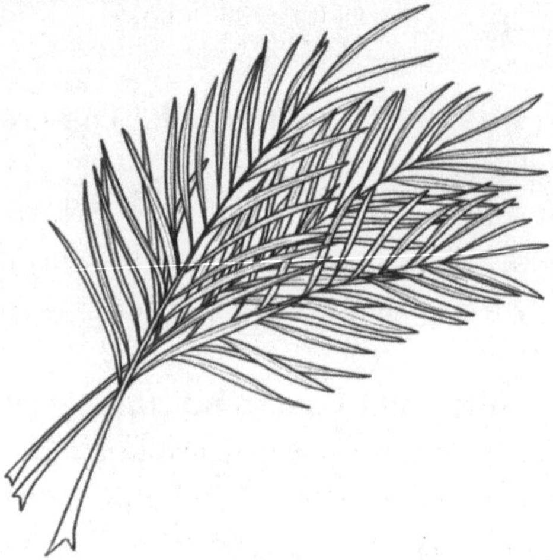

CHAPTER 12

Jesus Arrives in Jerusalem

After Jesus had brought Lazarus back to life again, and seen him settled back at home with his two sisters, he set off for the village of Ephraim, some fifteen miles or so north of Bethany. He wanted to have some time with his Father God, and prepare for the enormous task that lay ahead of him in Jerusalem. He knew that things were going to be tough.

After that break, he began to make his way through the towns and villages of the area, and back to his friends Mary, Martha, and Lazarus. Crowds of people followed him all the way. He told them parables, and he healed those who were ill. It was a slow journey, with many people needing help. He knew that he was working his way steadily toward

Jerusalem for the Passover festival, where his great mission would be completed.

Jesus arrived back in Bethany six days before Passover began. There his friends decided to put on a big banquet for him. All sorts of people came from around the area.

Bethany wasn't very far from Jerusalem, so a crowd of people set out from Jerusalem to see what would happen this time. They wanted to see Jesus, but they also wanted to see Lazarus. They thought it would be interesting to see someone who had been dead, but was now alive again.

Jerusalem was filling up with pilgrims for the Passover celebrations. This was usually the time when Neeko began to get excited in anticipation of the festival.

Since he had lost his elderly parents, he had made a habit of joining Josef and his family in their big house for the Passover meal on the evening of the first Sabbath of the festival. Then he would see quite a lot of them, and other friends, during the week of the festival, with plenty of feasting and good conversation.

This year, however, he was deeply troubled by what was going on with the Sanhedrin. They were a murderous lot. They were determined to trap Jesus and silence him. In fact, he heard that they were planning to kill Lazarus too.

Neeko decided to wander out to the gate on the eastern side of the city, through which the lambs would be coming ready for the feast. There were lots of people heading in the same direction. Many pilgrims were among them, all talking excitedly. They were carrying branches from the palm trees.

"What's going on?" he asked one family.

"Haven't you heard?" they replied. "It's Jesus of course. He is on his way into the city." Their little girl looked up at him.

"Have you met Jesus?" she asked.

"Yes, I have actually," answered Neeko.

"Would you like a branch to wave?" she asked. "You look a bit sad."

"No, thank you," answered Neeko. "Yes, I'm sorry. Yes, I am a bit sad. I will just watch. Thank you."

As he followed this little family, hurrying along excitedly ahead of him, he felt a pang of regret. How he would have loved to welcome Jesus in this way, but Neeko knew that Jesus was walking into a trap. He knew that there was a nest of poisonous snakes waiting for him in the city.

He walked on together with everyone else toward the Eastern Gate that led out of the city toward the Garden of Gethsemane and on toward Bethany beyond.

From his boyhood days, Neeko knew of a number of places along the walls where he could climb a narrow flight of stairs and look out over the wall. These lookout posts dated from the time when watchmen patrolled the city at night, to look out for enemy attack. Since the Romans had occupied the country, however, these lookout posts had not been used. The Romans had no need of them. They didn't worry about attack from outside. They knew that they were far more likely to have trouble from inside the city.

However, the boys of the city knew of these interesting lookout places. They liked to climb up and look out over the surrounding countryside and they would use them in their games. Neeko remembered such a place near the Eastern Gate.

As he approached the gate, following the crowds that were streaming out of the city to welcome Jesus, he could see ahead of him a group of Pharisees from the council, standing at the gate and looking important. Neeko didn't want to be standing with them, so he slipped into an alleyway, which led to the lookout post. Gathering up his robe, he climbed the narrow stone steps to the top of the wall. From this vantage point he was able to look out over the parapet. He could see the road winding its way across the Kidron valley and away to Bethany.

In the distance, he could see the crowds gathering and milling around, and calling out excitedly. They were too far away for him to hear exactly what they were calling, but he could just about make out a figure riding a donkey. He shielded his eyes with his hand to get a clearer view. The crowds were lining the road. They were waving branches and shouting.

Gradually, the figure on the donkey became clearer as he worked his way toward the city. Neeko was beginning to hear the words that the people were shouting.

"Hosanna. Blessed is he that comes in the name of the Lord."

"Blessed is the King of Israel."

"Peace in Heaven."

The children were joining in the celebration and waving their palm branches.

"Glory in the highest," they shouted. "Blessed is the coming Kingdom of our father David."

"Hosanna in the highest."

People were gathering more leaves and palm branches and laying them on the road. Some of them were taking off their coats and laying them down for the donkey to step on.

"What an amazing sight," said Neeko to himself. He thought of the little girl who had offered him a palm branch. He found himself reciting these words from the prophet Zechariah:

"Rejoice greatly, O daughter of Zion.
Shout, daughters of Jerusalem.
See, your king comes to you,
Righteous and having salvation,
Gentle, and riding on a donkey…
He will speak peace to the nations.
His rule will extend from sea to sea,
And from the river to the ends of the earth."

As the crowd began to enter the city, Neeko turned and came back down the steps. He walked thoughtfully homeward, wondering what would become of all this.

When he next took his seat on the Sanhedrin council, he heard that Jesus had once again gone into the Temple courts and turned out all the traders. The council were determined to get him and make an end of him, but they were unable to touch him. He was constantly surrounded by crowds of people listening to his teaching.

The next thing Neeko heard was that one of Jesus' disciples had been to see the chief priests and officers of the Temple guard. They had agreed to pay him thirty pieces of silver to show them where they could find Jesus alone.

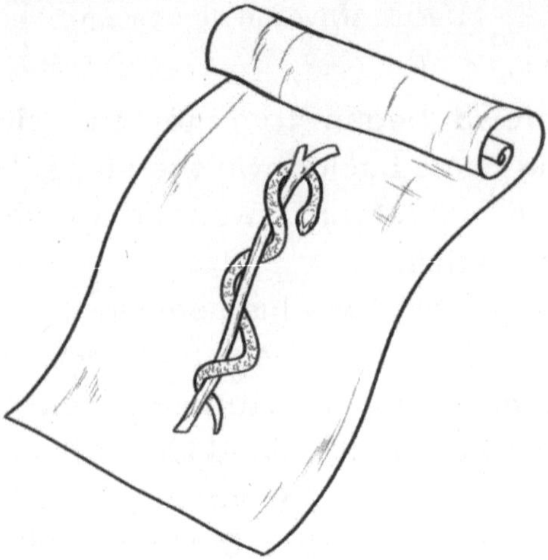

CHAPTER 13

The Snake on the Pole

Decisions were being made at speed and in secret, by small groups of council members. Nothing was being properly discussed in a full meeting of the Sanhedrin.

Neeko and Josef found themselves shut out of any discussions about Jesus. They just about managed to keep track of events by picking up fragments of information.

They heard that Jesus had been arrested by the Temple guard and brought before Annas, one of the chief priests. Then he had been taken to Caiaphas, the High Priest. Some carefully chosen members of the council were there too. All this had taken place at night, which everybody knew was against the Sanhedrin rules. It was obvious that things had been done like this to avoid any disagreement from people like Neeko and Josef, who were sympathetic to Jesus.

Now it was all too late. Jesus had been handed over to the Romans. A mob of troublemakers had been recruited to put pressure on Pilate, the Roman governor. So, Jesus had been condemned to be executed by crucifixion. There was nothing that could be done to stop it happening.

Jerusalem was full to bursting with pilgrims, who had come for the Passover festival. The Sanhedrin council wanted to get this "Jesus matter" cleared up and tidied away before the festival began. They wanted to enjoy the holiday, and the feasting with their friends and families. They had persuaded Pilate to get the crucifixion done well before sundown, because this was the preparation day for the first Sabbath of the festival.

Neeko knew the desolate place where the Romans conducted their executions. It was a high piece of ground outside the city wall. The locals called it "Skull Hill". Usually, it was deserted. Most people avoided the place, but today, as he came through the gate and looked up toward Skull Hill on the skyline, Neeko was amazed to see lots of people gathered there. High up above the crowd, stark against the sky, stood the wooden poles upon which the Romans strung their victims.

Three of these poles were occupied, and, as Neeko got nearer, he realized that the man hanging on the central one was Jesus. It was obvious that he had been tortured. He had been nailed to a cross-beam by his hands, and hoisted up high above the crowd. Then his feet had been nailed to the pole.

Neeko stood at the back of the crowd. Everyone was looking up at Jesus. Suddenly, Neeko remembered what Jesus had said to him during their night-time meeting a few years previously.

"In the same way that Moses set up a bronze snake on a pole in the desert in full view of the people, I will be lifted up high for everyone to see, so that those who look to me in faith will gain a new heavenly life that is eternal."

This is it, thought Neeko. *This is what he meant.*

At the front of the crowd, Neeko could see a group of chief priests and other members of the council. They were all laughing and joking, and shouting insults at Jesus. Others in the crowd were weeping. Neeko noticed the contrast between those who were hard-hearted and arrogant, and those soft-hearted souls who were touched by the tragedy of such a good man being tortured so brutally.

Hanging on the posts each side of Jesus were two criminals. A conversation was going on between the three men. Neeko moved a little closer to hear what they were saying. One of them turned his head toward Jesus.

"If you are so special," he yelled through gritted teeth, "why can't you save yourself, and while you're at it, save us too?" But the other one called back to him.

"Hold your tongue," he said. "Can't you see what's going on? You and me is 'ere because of what we've done. This fella, he's done nothing wrong."

Neeko was captivated by this conversation. Then the criminal turned his rough unshaven face up toward the face of Jesus.

"Lord," he said, struggling for breath, "think of me, when you get to be King in your new Kingdom." Despite the pain, Jesus looked across at the criminal with tenderness.

"Before this day is through," he said, "you will be walking with me in my Father's beautiful garden." The criminal turned his face away and bowed his head.

"Thanks," he said.

Neeko could see that Jesus divided these two men that were dying each side of him. One was cruel and bitter in the words he spoke to Jesus. The other understood and reached out for healing and blessing before he died. Neeko remembered the words of John at the Jordan river. "The one that comes after me will be like a farmer, sorting out his grain at harvest time. Wheat in one pile and chaff in the other."

Although it was the middle of the day, heavy black clouds rolled across the sky, shutting out the light. The sun itself seemed to sputter and die like a lamp running out of oil. Suddenly, the air went cold. A chilly breeze blew through the crowd. Neeko pulled his outer cloak more tightly around him, and tucked his hands into his sleeves. Then Jesus called out in a loud voice.

"Father, I give my spirit into your hands."

People were getting upset, and walking away to go home. Many of them were in tears. The centurion who was in charge of the execution could contain himself no longer.

"This really was a good man," he said reverently.

Neeko was just about to turn and walk away, when he heard a familiar voice behind him.

"What a dreadful sight." It was his friend Josef. They stood side by side, looking up at the silhouette of Jesus hanging there in the darkness.

"We have got to do something, Neeko," said Josef. "Before they dump his body among the rubbish down in the valley for the dogs and vultures to fight over."

"What can we do?" asked Neeko.

"My family has a private burial garden not far from here," answered Josef. "There's a brand new tomb with my name on it. We can put him in there. ... I'm going straight to Pilate to ask for the body."

"I will get some linen winding cloths and some embalming cream," said Neeko. "Let's give him a noble burial."

"Be back here as soon as you can," said Josef urgently. "We've got no time to lose."

The two men made their way in the darkness back into the city. Neeko went straight home.

"What's going on?" asked his servant as Neeko closed the door behind him. "Why is it so dark in the middle of the day, and so cold all of a sudden?"

"It's Jesus," replied Neeko. "They've crucified him. Listen, Amoz," he continued. "This is urgent. I need you to do a few things as quickly as you can. Go and hire a donkey, get one with pannier baskets. Hire him for the rest of the day. Then go to the perfumer." Neeko reached for his purse. "Get some embalming cream." He put some coins into Amoz's hand.

"Why gold, sir?" asked his servant.

"I want a lot, Amoz," instructed Neeko. "Get as much as you can. I am going to the cloth merchant for some linen winding cloths. Meet me back here as soon as you can. We don't want the Romans dumping the body on the rubbish tip to be eaten up by dogs."

While his servant went to fetch the embalming cream, Neeko set off through the darkened streets in search of some linen strips to wrap the body.

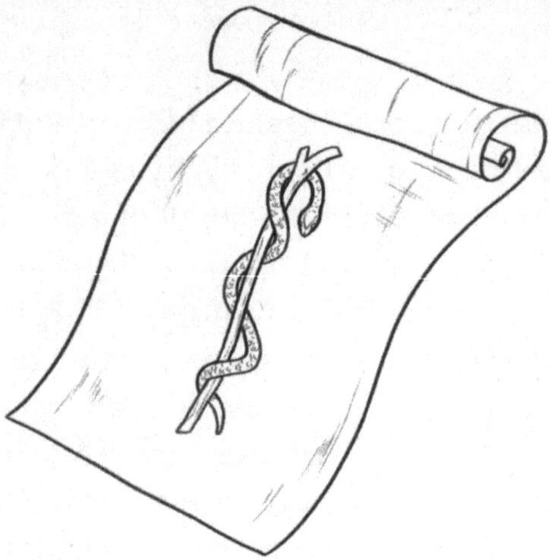

CHAPTER 14

Neeko and Josef Bury Jesus

It took a while for Neeko to get to the cloth merchants. The city was full of pilgrims, who had come up for the festival. Everyone was confused by the sudden darkness, and the chill that had descended upon them in the middle of the day. Amoz, too, took longer than expected to get the embalming cream. He bought two large, heavy jars full. He brought them in the baskets that hung each side of the donkey.

As soon as they had got back with their purchases, Neeko and his servant gathered the rest of the things they would need for cleaning the body, and set off with the donkey for Skull Hill.

When they got there, most of the crowd had gone, and the light was beginning to return. A few of Jesus' followers were still there, both men and women. They were in a state of shock and bewilderment. They stood at a distance, uncertain of what they should do.

Then Josef arrived with permission from Pilate to take the body. He was accompanied by the centurion, whom Pilate had summoned to confirm that Jesus was properly dead.

The men stood together, looking up at the body of Jesus, hanging high above them against the cloudy sky.

"I remember something that Jesus said," said Neeko. "That night when I went to talk with him, he said to me, 'In the same way that Moses set up a bronze snake on a pole in the desert in full view of the people, this body of mine will be lifted up high for everyone to see. Those who look to me in faith will gain a new heavenly life that is eternal.' This is what he was talking about, I am sure of it. This is where we get healed from that old snakebite, Josef."

There was a long and reverent silence, as they stood looking up, considering what Neeko had said. The centurion was the first to speak.

"I'm sorry, gentlemen," he said, "but we have orders to get rid of the bodies before sundown."

"Ah yes," said Josef. "The council wants everything tidied up, before the festival begins."

"Very good, sir," said the centurion. "I will get my men to lower the body for you. I will make sure they treat him with respect."

"You know what this means for us," said Neeko. "We will be unclean for the festival."

"Yes, I had thought of that," replied Josef. "Things are going to be very different for us from now on."

Once the body was down at ground level, the soldiers helped Josef and Neeko to get it wrapped in a cloth and laid over the back of the donkey. Then they made their way carefully down the hill. Amoz led the donkey, while Neeko and Josef steadied the body, until they arrived at the gate of Josef's family burial garden. Josef opened the gate in the stone wall, and they all passed through with the donkey and the body, into the peaceful surroundings of the secluded little garden.

The tombs had been cut out of the natural rock that formed the landscape of the garden. Most of them were closed, but one newly made tomb stood open. The great circular stone door was rolled back along its groove. A wooden wedge prevented it from rolling back down to close off the tomb.

They carefully lifted the body, and laid it on a large, flat rock, which stood in the middle of the garden for this very purpose. Some women from Jesus' followers stood at the gate looking in. They wanted to see where the body was placed, so that they could return later to add their own perfume to the grave-wrappings.

Then Neeko and Josef set about the task of cleaning and wrapping Jesus' body ready for burial.

This was a task normally done by women, but the two men were glad to be able to do it. They were grateful for an opportunity to show their respect to this great teacher, who had touched the lives of so many people.

Very little was said. Each man worked silently. They washed the body, and then began the long task of wrapping him with layer upon layer of linen. Between each layer, they smeared generous quantities of the expensive, fragrant embalming cream. They had never done such work before. They used so much linen and embalming cream that the whole thing looked more like an Egyptian mummy, than a normal Jewish burial.

When they had used up all the linen strips, only Jesus' face was visible. This they covered with the cream, then they gently laid a facecloth neatly over it.

Next, they lifted the wrapped body onto a wooden bier. This was like a wide plank with handles at each end. Neeko and Josef took the handles, and carried it into the tomb. There they eased the embalmed body off the flat wooden bier, and onto the stone shelf that ran along one side of the cave-like tomb. Then they came out into the late afternoon light of the garden. Together, the three men removed the wedge that held back the door. They carefully allowed it to trundle down its groove and into place over the doorway of the tomb. Then they fitted the wedge into the back of the stone and kicked it tightly into place.

They tidied up their things into the donkey's pannier baskets, and stood the bier back in its corner with the other gardening tools. Then they stood looking gloomily at one another.

"What now?" asked Neeko.

"Just wait, I suppose," replied Josef with a shrug.

"Something's going to happen," said Neeko. "I know it's not going to end like this."

"Well, at least we've got somewhere quiet to come and think of him," said Josef bleakly.

"I guess it's time we went home," said Neeko. "We shall have to get this donkey back before sundown."

The two women, who had watched everything from the gate, came into the garden.

"Excuse me, sir," said one of them to Josef. "Would you allow us to sit here for a while?"

Josef looked at the women, their weary faces stained with tears.

"Please, my dears, come in, and welcome. Stay as long as you like. It's been a tough day for all of us. Just remember to close the gate after you, when you leave."

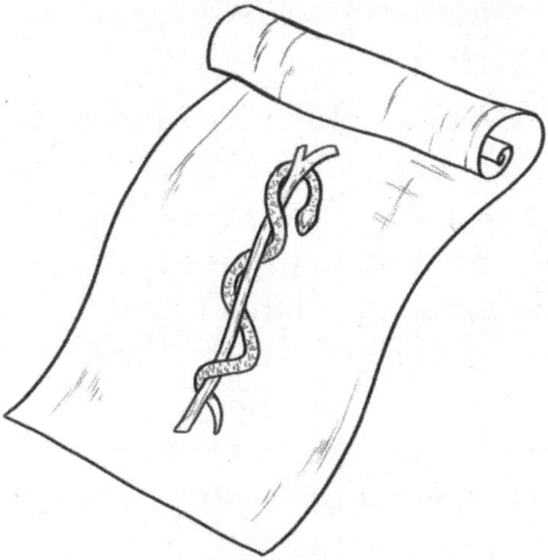

CHAPTER 15

The Wait

Neeko sent his servant ahead to take their things back to the house and return the donkey. Then he and Josef walked thoughtfully back into the city. The streets were full of pilgrims, all talking and laughing. The Passover festival was beginning to get under way. The whole city was full of the smell of cooking. Normally, Neeko would have been looking forward to joining Josef and his family for the Passover meal.

This year, things were going to be very different, but strangely, Neeko was not feeling sad. He remembered again the words of his old teacher. He could hear that lovely old warm voice.

"Remember this, boys. God is always looking for people who will trust him."

That evening was the beginning of the Sabbath. The Sanhedrin council did not normally sit on the Sabbath, but these were exceptional circumstances. The city gossips had been busy. News had reached them that Nicodemus and Josef had taken the body of Jesus. Somebody reported that Nicodemus' servant had spent an awful lot of money on embalming cream. Somebody else had seen them taking the body into Josef's family burial garden.

"That will make them unclean for seven days," said one of the Pharisees. "We don't want them sitting down with the rest of us on the council."

"In my view, these two should be permanently removed from the Sanhedrin council," said another. "They have clearly been corrupted by this Jesus fellow, and his teaching."

Then someone commented, with a sneer, that there were certain ways of excluding people permanently, and everybody laughed, and one or two men clapped.

Then one of the senior priests stood up and addressed the council.

"Gentlemen of the Sanhedrin," he began. "When Jesus of Nazareth was alive, he predicted that he would die and then come back to life again. I have a feeling that these two ex-colleagues of ours are up to no good. What if they are planning to stage some sort of stunt? It is unthinkable that they should go to so much trouble over this imposter's remains, and then make themselves unclean on the eve of the Passover festival. In my opinion, it is all very suspicious."

Then one of the chief priests spoke up.

"I think it would be wise to send a delegation to Pilate. Explain the seriousness of the situation and ask for a guard to be stationed at the tomb. It will be in the interest of the Romans to prevent any false stories being cooked up by this fellow's disciples."

So it was that a large group of chief priests and Pharisees turned up at Pilate's residence. He heard their story. Then, with a resigned sigh, he ordered that a squad of soldiers should go with them to the graveyard.

To make doubly sure, the council members took with them the great Sanhedrin seal and a quantity of sealing wax so that no one could tamper with the door of the tomb. It was, of course, against the Pharisees' rules to melt wax or to stamp it with a seal on the Sabbath day, but as they had agreed many times, these were exceptional circumstances.

It was a strange sight for the pilgrims to see, this large group of religious men marching through the busy, narrow streets of Jerusalem accompanied by a squad of Roman soldiers on the first Sabbath day of the festival.

This odd company of men made their way out of the city, to Josef's family burial garden. There, the council members persuaded the soldiers to do the work of melting the wax and putting great dobs of the stuff where the stone door closed onto the tomb. Before each dob of wax had hardened, the Sanhedrin seal was pressed firmly into it. Nobody would dare tamper with this now.

The council members left the soldiers on guard by the tomb. One stood at the gate, with instructions to let no one in. Then the council members walked back into the city, to continue celebrating the Passover festival. They all felt that they had done a good job of sorting out this messy Jesus business once and for all. But God had a few surprises in store for the members of the Sanhedrin, and especially for those who worked as priests at the Temple.

That night, Neeko had difficulty sleeping. He had seen such terrible things. He couldn't get them out of his mind.

The following day, which was the Sabbath, he decided to spend the time quietly reading the Scriptures. Strangely enough, he didn't feel low. He was sure that something was going to happen.

Reading the Scriptures was always comforting for him, but after what he had experienced, it was particularly so. He unrolled the scroll that contained the writing of the great prophet Isaiah, and began to read. He found some amazing words, which, although they had been written many hundreds of years before, seemed to describe exactly what Neeko had seen over the past few days.

> *"He was despised and rejected by men.*
> *He was a man full of sorrow,*
> *And was no stranger to suffering.*
> *He was wounded for the evil things that we had done,*
> *Beaten up for our mistakes.*
> *It was his wounds that brought us healing."*

"That's just like Moses' snake on the pole, bringing healing to the people from the snakebite," said Neeko to himself. Then he continued reading.

> *"His body should have been dumped with the criminals,*
> *But rich men were involved with his death."*

Wow. That could almost be referring to Josef and me, thought Neeko. Then he read these words:

> *"After he has suffered, he will wake up*
> *To the light of a new dawn.*
> *He will see the fruit of all his troubles,*
> *And he will be satisfied."*

Neeko knew these words well. He had often puzzled over their meaning, but now they made so much sense. They filled him with hope that seemed to rise up within him. Despite the dreadful events of the past few days, he had a strong feeling that things were going to turn out well.

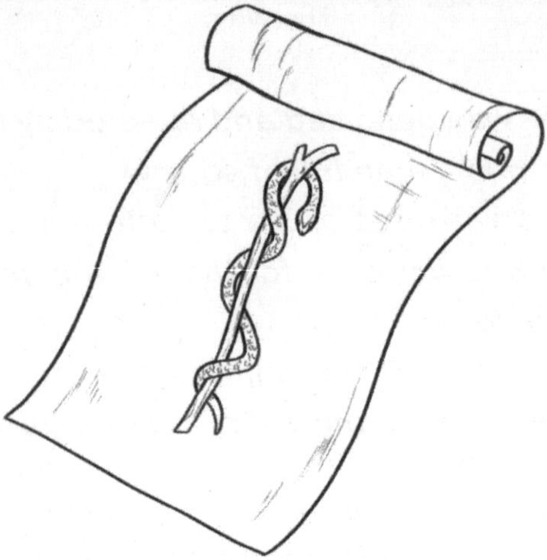

CHAPTER 16

Seismic Happenings

That night Neeko slept soundly. It was long past his usual time of rising, when he was woken by someone banging on the house door. Then Amoz put his head round the curtain that closed off his bedchamber.

"Excuse me, sir. It's Josef. He is very excited, sir. I think something has happened."

"Alright Amoz, give me a few minutes, and I will be with him," said Neeko sleepily. "Tell him to step inside for a minute."

Neeko poured a little water into his washing bowl. He gave his face a quick splash and dried it on a towel. He pulled on some clothes, buckled his sandals, and went out to meet Josef.

As soon as he saw him, Neeko knew that something amazing had taken place.

"Neeko, you must come," Josef said. "Get your hat and coat, and come with me."

"Give me a chance," replied Neeko. "I have only just got out of bed."

Neeko reached for the jug and poured himself a drink. He peered at his friend over the rim of his cup. He had never before seen Josef so wound up.

"Come on, Neeko," said Josef, reaching for the door. "You won't believe what has been going on down at the burial garden."

Neeko wiped his mouth with the back of his hand. He pulled on his coat, and followed Josef out onto the street. Josef was already striding off. Neeko had to run to catch up with him.

"So, what's all this about?" asked Neeko once he had caught up with his friend.

"I will have to show you. You won't believe me otherwise," said Josef, walking on purposefully.

Eventually, they arrived at Josef's little family burial garden. The gate in the wall was standing open, but it was at rather a strange angle. Neeko followed Josef into the garden. The two men stood just inside the gate, and stared at the scene.

"This is not how we left things," observed Neeko. "It looks as if a herd of cattle has rampaged through the place."

There were cracks in the garden wall. A lot of its stones had fallen out, and were lying on the floor. The wooden bier and the garden tools, which usually stood neatly in the corner, were lying in a disorganized heap. Some of the trees had fallen over, and lay with their roots showing. The flat stone table that stood in the middle of the garden was no longer lying flat. It was tipped up, with one corner in the air.

What really grabbed their attention, however, was the tomb itself, where they had so carefully placed the body of Jesus only a few days before. The circular stone door had been rolled back, and had dropped out of the channel in which it should have rolled. Great cracks had appeared in the stonework around the door.

Neeko followed Josef across to the tomb, stepping over the fragments of stone that littered the path.

"There must have been some sort of earthquake," said Josef. "But come and have a look inside. You must see this, Neeko."

The two men ducked through the doorway of the tomb, and stood together surveying the scene. There on the stone shelf lay the embalmed wrappings, just as they had left them. They were still in exactly the same place. Their shape was unchanged, but they were empty. The body had gone. Neeko took a step closer, and peered inside at the body-shaped cavity left in the hollow wrappings. Next to these empty grave clothes, lying neatly folded on the stone shelf, was the facecloth that they had laid on Jesus' face.

Neeko and Josef stood for a while in silence, wondering at the clear evidence that lay before their eyes. There was no doubt. An amazing miracle had taken place. Neeko began to recite the words upon which he had been pondering the day before.

> *"After he has suffered, he will wake up*
> *To the light of a new dawn.*
> *He will see the fruit of all his troubles,*
> *And he will be satisfied."*

"Is that Isaiah?" asked Josef.

"Yes, it is," replied Neeko. "Isaiah saw all of this."

Neeko and Josef came out of the tomb into the light of the little family burial garden, now in need of a good tidy-up. Neeko looked again at the tomb from the outside. His attention was drawn to the broken seals that lay among the rubble on the floor. He picked up a piece, and turned it over in his hand.

"What's this?" he asked. "It looks like the Sanhedrin seal. What's that doing here?"

"They came yesterday," said Josef. "They brought soldiers from Pilate to guard the tomb. They sealed the stone door, so that no one could tamper with it."

"Working on the Sabbath, eh?" Neeko said with a wry smile.

"They have bribed the guards to tell everybody that his disciples came and stole the body," said Josef. "And there's another thing. You know the great embroidered curtain, that divides the Holy-place from the Most-Holy-place in the Temple? Well, that has been torn, from top to bottom."

"That's going to take some explaining," said Neeko, looking down at the broken piece of seal in his hand. He knew that neither he, nor Josef, would ever again be allowed to take their seats on the Sanhedrin council. He tossed the piece of seal onto a pile of broken stones.

"This is going to be a new dawn for us too," said Josef.

"You are right, my friend," said Neeko, looking directly at Josef. "We have seen too much. We can never go back to the way things were.

"We have seen the body of Jesus strung up on a pole for all to see, just like Moses' snake in the desert. We have seen a curtain of darkness miraculously pulled across the sky in the middle of the day. Now we have seen these empty wrappings in the tomb.

"We have seen the stone door rolled away from the opening of the tomb, and great cracks in the solid rock of the tomb itself. These stones are shouting out their message. How can we ignore them, Josef? There can be no doubt. Jesus from Nazareth must be God's promised Messiah. We cannot keep this evidence to ourselves."

The two men stood in silence for a long time. Both of them knew that they faced a completely new chapter in their lives. Neeko spoke first.

“I am going back to school, Josef. I need to read the old Scriptures all over again. I have found a new teacher. He is far greater than my dear old teacher, Rabbi Jakov.”

“Well, in that case, I think we need to find you a wife,” said Josef, with a smile. Neeko looked at him quizzically. “One who can bake good spiced cakes,” added Josef.

APPENDIX

Mrs Jakov's Spiced Cakes

Ingredients

200 grams (7 ounces) pitted dates
20 grams (1 ounce) crystallized ginger, chopped
2 eggs, lightly beaten
100 grams (3½ ounces) ground rice
150 grams (5 ounces) ground almonds
40 grams (1½ ounces) chopped almonds
¼ teaspoon bicarbonate of soda
1½ teaspoons mixed spice
Pinch of salt

Heat oven to 170 degrees C (gas mark 3).

Line two baking trays with baking parchment, or brush them with oil.

Chop the dates. Put them in a saucepan with 60 ml. (2 fl. oz.) water and slowly warm them to soften them. Mash them with a potato masher. Then allow them to cool.

Add the beaten eggs.

Weigh out all the other ingredients, add them to the mixture in the saucepan, and mix thoroughly.

Space out dessert spoonfuls of the mixture onto the baking trays. Gently flatten them to about 1 cm (½ in.) thickness.

Bake for about fifteen minutes, then cool them on a wire rack.

Store in an airtight tin. Will keep for two or three days (unless you have a classful of hungry boys, in which case they will keep for about five minutes).

ALSO AVAILABLE

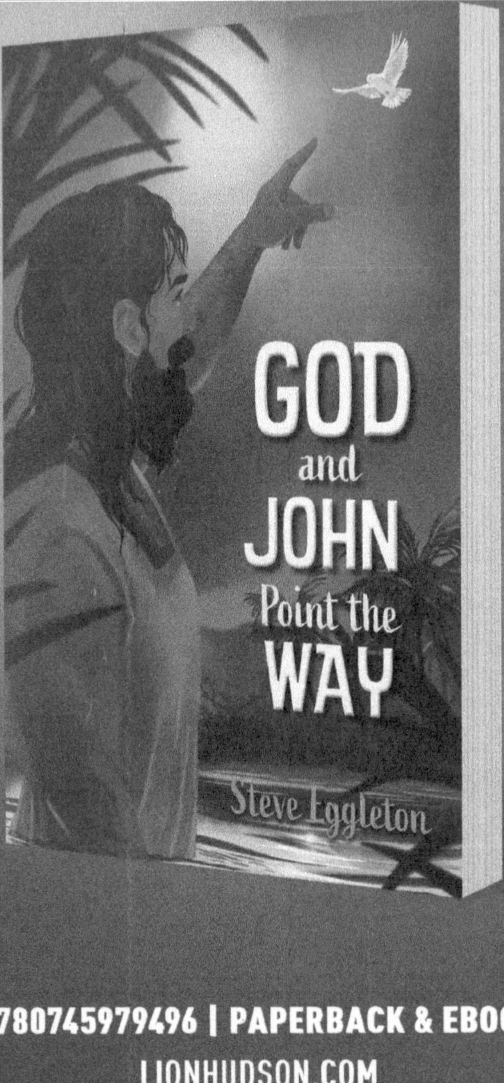

9780745979496 | PAPERBACK & EBOOK

LIONHUDSON.COM